LEARN TO CYCLE IN AMSTERDAM

LEARN TO CYCLE IN AMSTERDAM

XING CHEN

XPAT Scriptum Publishers

XPAT Scriptum Publishers
Van Boetzelaerlaan 153
2581 AR The Hague
The Netherlands
Tel.: +31 (0)70 306 33 10 / +31 (0)10 427 10 22
info@xpat.nl

© Photography: Kevin McPeake, Shirley Agudo, Xing Chen,
Ben Deiman, Tim Bleeker.
On the cover: Xing Chen, photo by Kevin McPeake

Final text editing: Stephanie Dijkstra
Design and Layout: Bram Vandenberge, www.igraph.be

ISBN   978 94 6319 076 3
NUR   461

Visit us at:
www.xpat.nl
www.scriptum.nl
www.hollandbooks.nl

TABLE OF CONTENTS

INTRODUCTION

30

CHAPTER 1
BICYCLES, ACCESSORIES, PURCHASING, AND MAINTENANCE

48

CHAPTER 2
ROAD SIGNS

CHAPTER 3
TIPS AND
ETIQUETTE FOR
CYCLISTS

**CHAPTER 4
PREDICTING
THE BEHAVIOUR
OF OTHER
ROAD USERS**

142

CHAPTER 5
WEATHER, CLOTHING, AND ROAD CONDITIONS

A typical, bustling intersection in the heart of Amsterdam

INTRODUCTION

Amsterdam, the 'bicycle capital' of the world

Amsterdam is one of the most bicycle-friendly cities in the world.[1,2] There are approximately 847,000 bicycles for a population of 800,000 people[3] – in other words, the city has more bicycles than people. Visitors quickly realise that it is cyclists, not car drivers, who rule the road, and pedestrians are cautioned to check for bicycles when crossing the street, or risk getting run over. Indeed, travelling by car can be onerous, particularly in the busy centre. Speed limits, narrow one-way streets, and the limited availability of parking spaces conspire to discourage people from driving, and short trips are often quicker by bicycle than by car.[4]

Much of the local population gets around by bicycle on a regular basis. 78% of Amsterdammers own a bike (many people own more than one)[3]; 57% of them use their bike everyday; and 43% ride their bike to work.[5] An estimated 223 million journeys are made by bicycle in Amsterdam per year, which works out to an average of 613,000 journeys (or the equivalent of a distance of 2 million km) per day.[5]

The cycling infrastructure in the city is extensive, to say the least. Cyclists have access to dedicated cycle paths, and they are also allowed on roads with a 30-km/h speed limit (which applies to 90% of all the roads in Amsterdam[3]). Annually, the city spends approximately €15 million on cycling infrastructure, yielding a formidable network of 767 km of cycle paths and bicycle lanes in Amsterdam alone, of which 513 km are dedicated cycle paths.[3]

This investment more than pays off, however, as cycling leads to savings on road infrastructure for cars and public transport, amounting to an estimated €40 million per year. A single car parking space can accommodate the equivalent of 15 bikes,[3] and there are approximately 250,000 bicycle parking spots scattered across the city. To serve the needs of cyclists,

Amsterdam has 140 bicycle shops (or almost one shop per square kilometre on average), as well as 29 bicycle rental businesses.[3]

Due to the rising popularity of 'cycling as a lifestyle' in cities throughout the world, and Amsterdam's reputation as a 'model city' in terms of both cycling infrastructure and the proportion of trips that are made by bike, foreign policy makers often pay visits to transport planners from the local municipality. To meet

Each year, 12,000 to 15,000 bicycles are removed from the city's canals[6]

this demand for expertise and to further promote the use of bicycles in urban areas, an organisation known as CycleSpace was established, with the support of the City of Amsterdam. Its role is to carry out innovative research on cycling, organise events such as workshops, knowledge-sharing sessions and cycling tours, and spread the passion for cycling to other countries and cities.[7,8] In 2016, the city even appointed its first cycling ambassador to a semi-official position known as the 'Bicycle Mayor', whose task is to facilitate communication between City Hall officials, cyclists, cycling advocacy groups, and the general public.[9,10] Hence, the city's reputation is well deserved!

Who will benefit from this book?

Cycling involves a combination of motor control, planning, mental agility, and practice. This essential guide covers numerous aspects of learning how to ride your bicycle amidst the hustle and bustle of the small but dynamic city of Amsterdam, while being surrounded by dense vehicular traffic, pedestrians, cyclists, motorcyclists, and a variety of other road users. It will introduce you to the basic rules of the road, allowing you to develop and refine your road etiquette. You will learn to predict the behaviour of other road users, plan your movements several steps in advance, and adjust your behaviour as the need arises. The practical, in-depth information provided by this guide will help you to gain confidence and deal with unexpected situations with grace and quick thinking.

This book is meant for readers who already know how to ride a bicycle, and who feel comfortable when cycling in quiet, pedestrian- and bicycle-friendly areas with low car densities. It does not cover the technicalities of learning to cycle from the very beginning. You may have learnt to ride a bicycle during your childhood or teenage years, in a relatively safe environment such as a residential neighbourhood or park. However, when it comes to navigating through busy, built-up areas with high levels of traffic, such as that seen in the centre of Amsterdam, these basic cycling skills are not enough. In order to cycle confidently through crowded streets, one needs to acquire additional skills, and gain detailed knowledge about traffic rules and road user behaviour. In 'Learning to Cycle in Amsterdam', we will focus on the acquisition and development of these skills and knowledge. Furthermore, this guide is aimed at bicycle riders, not motorcyclists.

The benefits of cycling

Cycling is thought to offer numerous mental and health benefits.[11,12] Many people enjoy spending their time outdoors, commuting in the fresh air, instead of taking public transport or driving. As a form of exercise, cycling is relatively low-impact and exerts less repetitive strain on the joints than activities such as running, as part of your body weight is borne by the bicycle. At a practical level, it allows you to travel at speeds of around 15 km/h or more, covering distances more quickly than by foot. You can adjust the degree of physical exertion, depending on the type of bicycle you ride and your gear settings. On warm days, the breeze created while cycling has a cooling effect, whereas on cold days, the physical exertion helps to keep you warm. Commuting by bicycle allows you to bypass unexpected disruptions in the public transport system and eliminates the wait for buses, metros, trains, and trams, making the duration of one's commute more predictable. It also permits easy access to areas that are not well served by public transport.

The downsides of cycling

As you can likely imagine, cycling is not always a bed of roses. The weather can affect visibility and road conditions significantly, sometimes making the ride harder or less enjoyable. You may need to adjust your clothing depending on the weather, and perhaps bring a change of clothes along with you. If you cycle for long durations, you may notice that your appetite increases because you expend more energy. Furthermore, if you get a puncture or a flat tire, this will require attention and result in delays.

Importantly, you need to stay alert to surrounding traffic. Unexpected events, such as road diversions and obstacles, require quick reflexes and may force you to alter your route. Also note that one encounters a wide spectrum of road users on the street – from the courteous and friendly, to the flat-out unpleasant. And while traffic accidents are rare, all road users run the risk of being involved in one. In this book, rather than glossing over the hardships, I strive for a realistic, honest portrayal of the cycling experience in Amsterdam, presenting the pros as well as the cons, so that you will be better equipped to deal with challenges if and when they arise.

Sharing the road with others

Although bicycles are a dominant mode of transport in Amsterdam and cyclists benefit from their own cycle lanes and traffic light system, cyclists must share the road with all other forms of traffic – cars, trucks, buses, trams, pedestrians, tourists, horses, and each other.

The difference between cycling in a quiet park and cycling in the centre of Amsterdam is analogous to the difference between driving a car on a quiet road in the middle of the desert and driving a car in the middle of a big city. You have to take numerous factors into account, such as the weather, road conditions, and visibility. In particular, you need to be

A cyclist shares the bicycle
path with a horse rider

A glimpse of the diversity of
road users in Amsterdam

able to predict the behaviour of other road users, including drivers of motorised vehicles, pedestrians, and other cyclists. This requires, first of all, a basic grasp of the rules of the road – and not just the rules that pertain exclusively to cyclists. You have to be able to quickly identify subsets of people and vehicles, and guess what they are about to do – are they veterans at navigating the crowded streets, or are they newcomers? Are they going to block your way or let you pass?

Organisation of this book

This book is organised into five chapters, with some overlap between closely related topics. The first chapter, 'Bicycles, accessories, purchasing, and maintenance' starts with your gear – it describes the most popular types of bicycles, how to purchase a bicycle, and the most commonly used bicycle accessories. The second chapter, 'Road signs', dives into the rules of the road, providing you with underlying knowledge of what is legal and what is not. The third chapter, 'Tips and etiquette for cyclists', is a practical guide that covers a range of situations on the road, with advice on how to react appropriately. The fourth chapter, 'Predicting the behaviour of other road users', describes the characteristics of various groups of road users, and how to anticipate their actions. The fifth chapter, 'Weather, clothing, and road conditions', covers slightly more advanced topics, such as dealing with bad weather and difficult road surface conditions. Throughout the book, you will find that some topics are mentioned within more than one section. If a topic is described in detail elsewhere in the text, a reference is made to the relevant section.

The author enjoying the Dutch summer

A WORD FROM THE AUTHOR

I first learnt to ride a bicycle when I was in my pre-teens, at around the age of 11 or 12. I lived in a quiet suburban neighbourhood, with relatively few cars and lots of winding roads. Children played freely in the streets, and cars drove past at a leisurely speed. Throughout my teens and early twenties, I continued cycling occasionally, for recreation or on short commutes, through quiet neighbourhoods or small cities. Then, at the age of 28, I moved to Amsterdam.

Initially, when I started cycling in a crowded environment, I didn't quite understand how the traffic worked (aside from the most obvious signals, such as traffic lights). I was never quite sure whether I had the 'right of way', and often worried about whether I needed to swerve or stop abruptly to accommodate someone, while increasing the risk of colliding with someone else. Simply put, I was afraid – afraid of causing an accident, being in an accident, or looking like a dangerously clueless cyclist in front of a crowd of veterans.

At the beginning, I thought that the solution was to always move fast. My reasoning was that the less time I spent in any given spot, the lower my chances of getting in someone's way. As time went by and I became more familiar with the rules of the road and the behaviour of other road users, I realised that this philosophy was flawed. The road system is set up to accommodate cyclists of varying speeds, including those moving at lower speeds, and there is no mandate that requires you to move faster than what feels safe and comfortable for you.

Seared into my memory is an incident that occurred within the first few months of my move to Amsterdam. I was crossing a road in the city centre, and attempting to merge into the bicycle lane. However, a continuous stream of cyclists was flowing past, and I was stuck on the car lane, with cars rapidly approaching. I didn't know what to do, and I certainly didn't want to get hit by a car, so I tried to insert myself into the fast-moving stream of cyclists. Another cyclist, on a collision course with me, called out a warning. Somehow, we avoided each other and I carried on, shaken and chastened. Although it was a seemingly small event, which fortunately did not end badly, it left my heart pounding. I asked myself how it happened, why it happened, and how I could avoid such a situation in the future. I realised, with hindsight, that I had probably chosen the wrong time to attempt to cross the road – I had waited until the road was clear of cars, but I had not checked to see whether the density of cyclists was low enough to allow me to merge into the cycle lane just next to the car lane.

On another occasion, I was attempting to cross a two-lane road, and was in the middle of the street when an ambulance approached at high speed, along the side of the road that I had already traversed. Assuming that the ambulance would carry on along the lane behind me, I continued to cross the second lane, when the ambulance suddenly switched lanes, driving along the wrong side of the road, and heading straight at me. The ambulance swerved and managed to avoid me, and I was left looking after it in shock. I realised that I had never learnt how to share the road with an ambulance before, and did not know how to react in such a situation. Although I knew that ambulances and emergency vehicles had the right of way, I had not realised that they may

sometimes break traffic rules and that other road users had to stop and yield completely.

These stories illustrate several points that I will make repeatedly throughout this book. Firstly, cycling in a bustling city takes practice. It cannot and should not be rushed. If you feel nervous in traffic, there is no point in expecting too much of yourself and thinking that you need to go as fast and as hard as all the local 'experts'. If you feel your heart beating after a close brush with other road users, take a break – not long enough to lose your momentum, but certainly enough to catch your breath and calm down, before trying again.

Secondly, the road is governed by all kinds of written and unwritten rules, some of which can be deduced through common sense, but many others of which are arbitrary and have to be learnt one way or another. Some people feel that all that is needed is to go out and 'just do it'. This is certainly the approach that I adopted when I started to cycle in Amsterdam. But think about it – why are automobile drivers required to study traffic rules and pass theory exams before they are allowed to drive independently? This is to accelerate the learning process and ensure that drivers abide by a common set of rules from the get-go, rather than learning them slowly and painfully by trial and error, or not at all. Although cyclists often have dedicated cycle paths and they do not move as fast as drivers of other motorised vehicles on average, they are still road users in constant interaction with the rest of the traffic. Detailed knowledge of road etiquette and conventions is what differentiates newcomers from long-time residents.

Thirdly, until you have been exposed to a variety of situations and grown familiar with the rules, you are bound to make some mistakes. Do not let that deter you – everyone goes through this process when learning to cycle in a crowded, stressful environment. If you have not had the benefit of making and learning from such mistakes during childhood, then it is nearly inevitable that you will make them later on. Remember to celebrate your achievements and improved cycling skills, and put the past behind you, even as you continue to learn from it.

Fourthly and finally, as you practice, you will become better at predicting what is going to happen next. You will gradually become familiar with the layout of the city, recognise roads, and learn to predict the behaviour of the people around you. Importantly, this will allow you to see several steps ahead – you will go from having to focus all of your attention on the upcoming task (whether that is crossing the road safely, merging with traffic, or signalling a turn), to being able to plan two or more steps ahead and adjust your behaviour to your rapidly changing surroundings.

USEFUL PHRASES

Goedemorgen	Good morning
Goedemiddag	Good afternoon
Goedenavond	Good evening
Pardon, mevrouw/meneer	Excuse me, madam/sir
Weet u waar de ___ straat/ weg/laan is?	Do you know where the ___ Street/ road/lane is?
Waar is de ___?	Where is the ___?
Dank u wel	Thank you
Sorry	Sorry
Pardon	Excuse me
Dit is mijn fiets	This is my bicycle
Fietspad	Bicycle path
Dus geen snor- en bromfietsen	No scooters allowed
Fietsenstalling	Bicycle parking space
Rekken/vakken	Bicycle racks/spaces
Geen fietsen plaatsen	No parking for bicycles
Fietsen worden verwijderd	Bicycles will be removed

Fietsen toegestaan	Bicycles allowed
Fietsers uitgezonderd	Cyclists exempted
Rechtsaf voor fietsers vrij	Bicycles are allowed to turn right when the light is red
Pas op!	Beware!
Wacht tot het rode licht is gedoofd. Er kan nog een trein komen	Wait until the red light stops flashing. Another train may be approaching
Omleiding	Diversion
Werkverkeer op pad	Work vehicles on the cycle path
Drempels	Road bumps
Veerooster/wildrooster	Cattle grid
Slecht wegdek	Poor road surface
Stadsfiets	City bike
Vouwfiets	Folding bike
Bakfiets	Bicycle cart for transporting goods
Baby mee	Baby carrier
Ringslot	Wheel lock
Kettingslot	Chain lock
Beugelslot	U-lock
Vouwslot	Folding lock

CHAPTER 1

BICYCLES, ACCESSORIES, PURCHASING, AND MAINTENANCE

Types of bicycles

Broadly speaking, a 'city bike' is one that is suitable for use in a city environment. It is sturdily built, allowing it to withstand the elements and survive minor crashes. It is designed for riding on even (preferably paved) surfaces, with tires that provide a moderate amount of grip. The height of the handlebars is fairly high relative to the seat, allowing the rider to sit in an upright position and maintain a clear view of surrounding traffic. As these bicycles are often used for commuting, they tend to be outfitted with accessories such as a sturdy rack, panniers (a type of bicycle bag), or baskets. Mudguards and skirt guards are often used to protect the rider's clothing from splashes and mud, and to prevent oil stains from the bicycle chain, allowing users to wear ordinary 'street' clothes. Many variations on the city bike are available, yielding slightly different seating postures, ranging from the upright to the semi-upright. They may come with hand brakes or foot brakes (also known as 'coaster brakes'), and have a single gear or multiple gears. Many of them are outfitted with a kickstand, although some are not.

These features distinguish city bicycles from sports bicycles, such as road bikes, which are lighter in build and require the rider to

An *omafiets*, with a casing
around the bicycle chain

Cycling through the centre
on a 'typical' city bike

adopt a more crouched-over posture. In order to minimise the weight of the bicycle, sports bicycles typically come with few or no accessories. Riders of sports bicycles tend to move at higher speeds and perspire more heavily while cycling, hence they often wear specialised cycling clothes and a helmet.

In Amsterdam, many cyclists ride a type of city bicycle known as an *omafiets* or an *opafiets* (meaning 'grandma bike' or 'grandpa bike'), which is popularly thought to be representative of a 'Dutch' bike. It is characterised by a sturdy frame, with handlebars that curve backwards and allow the rider to adopt a comfortable, upright posture, with good visibility over the surroundings. The chain is typically enclosed in casing to protect it from the elements, and to protect the rider's clothing from oil stains. They are also frequently outfitted with a wheel lock around the back wheel, which can be used in combination with a heavy-duty chain.

Folding bikes are compact, lightweight, foldable bicycles, which can be expanded to their full size or collapsed to a fraction of that size in a matter of seconds. The advantages of using a folding bike include being able to take it for free on public transport, whether on the bus, train, metro, or tram, and being able to keep it unobtrusively indoors instead of leaving it chained up outside.

Riding a light, compact folding bike

Brakes

Most bicycles have either foot brakes or hand brakes. Hand brakes are controlled using the hands, and there may be one for each wheel, or just one for one of the wheels. With hand brakes, it is possible to brake while keeping your feet off the pedals and positioned closer to the ground, in anticipation for your stop.

Foot brakes (also known as 'coaster brakes') are operated by pedalling backwards with the feet. Foot brakes engage only the back wheel, so some bicycles with coaster brakes also come with a hand brake for the front wheel. City bikes are often equipped with coaster brakes, although this is not always the case. Unlike in bikes with hand brakes, the pedals cannot be spun backwards freely, as that would engage the brake.

Foot brakes are rarely seen outside the Netherlands, and take some practice to get used to. When decelerating, you need to know how much pressure to exert with your feet, in order to decelerate at the right speed. When coasting down a hill or negotiating a bend, you will likely need to apply light, constant pressure. When coming to an abrupt stop, you need to brake strongly, and then quickly place your feet on the ground and/or jump down from the bike, in order to avoid falling over. As the pedals cannot be spun around freely, some extra planning is required.

This cyclist uses a set of hand brakes

For example, when coming to a temporary stop (such as at a traffic light), it helps to position the pedals such that one of them is at a high level at the moment that you come to a standstill. You may then step down upon it to accelerate, when it is time to take off again. If your pedals are not positioned at an optimal height for exerting a downward force, you will need to push yourself forward with one or both of your feet, and keep your balance and momentum while pedalling, until you build up sufficient speed. For this reason, you sometimes see people get off to a slow start, e.g. at traffic lights. For more information about braking in general, refer to the section on 'Slowing down and braking' in Chapter 3.

Gears

Amsterdam's city centre is fairly flat, with the occasional bridge curving over a canal. For short commutes within the city, it is not essential for your bicycle to have multiple gears. You may occasionally need to build up some momentum and/or stand on the pedals and use your body weight to generate extra force when crossing a bridge. Nevertheless, gears can come in handy, particularly for the steeper bridges. Many city bikes are equipped with only a single gear, although some now come with multiple gears.

Similarly, if one or more of your hands are occupied and this prevents you from standing on the pedals, or if you cycle in poor weather or in the presence of strong winds, it is useful to be able to switch gears. For longer commutes, such as to the outskirts of Amsterdam, you may traverse overhead bridges, with long, steep inclines, and gears can make the journey faster and easier. For more information about switching gears and adjusting your speed, refer to the section, 'Speeds and gears' in Chapter 3.

Gears are useful for climbing the bridges over the canals

Buying a bike

There are many brands of bikes available, the most popular of which include Giant, Batavus, and Gazelle for city bikes, and Brompton for folding bikes. Secondhand bicycles can be found in bicycle stores or through online classified advertisements such as Marktplaats.nl, and can be bought for as little as €50-150. New bicycles may be purchased from bicycle stores, and prices typically start at €200 and up. In some areas of the city, illegal vendors are known to hawk stolen bikes for extremely low prices, on the order of €10. Note that it is a criminal offence to purchase a stolen bike.[13] If a bicycle has unique identifying information, such as a theft prevention chip number or a frame number, it is possible to consult an online registry (https://fdr.rdw.nl) to check whether it has previously been reported as stolen. For more information on unique identifying information, refer to the section on 'Parking, locks, and theft' in Chapter 3. If you wish to report a stolen bike, you can call the police, using either the regular phone number at 0900 8844, or the anonymous hotline at 0800 7000.

Renting a bike

You can rent a bicycle from one of the many bicycle stores scattered throughout the city. These typically charge hourly or daily rates, and the bicycles come with a sturdy lock.

The city also has several bicycle-sharing schemes, such as the Urbee rental scheme which serves a broad region of Amsterdam with its fleet of electric bicycles, and the Hello-Bike rental scheme which serves primarily the Zuidas district. Both of these schemes rely on a mobile app booking system, allowing users to locate and book a bicycle in advance of their ride or on the spot. The rental bicycles are equipped with smart locks, hence users can pick up their bike from a station along the street, instead of visiting a brick-and-mortar store. The Hello-Bike rental scheme offers sturdy, red, upright-style bicycles, and prices start at €1 per hour (www.hello-bike.net), while Urbee offers e-bikes (which can be used with or

Exploring the city centre on rental bikes

without the assistive motor), and prices start at €1-2 per hour, depending on whether you choose a subscription plan or pay-as-you-go (www.urbee.nl). One of the main challenges faced by bicycle-sharing schemes the world over is to ensure an adequate supply of bicycles at each of the stations, as bicycles tend to accumulate in certain areas, while becoming scarce in others. To solve this, most bicycle-sharing schemes either require users to return their bike to the same station as that from which they picked it up, or impose an additional fee if the bicycle is returned to a different station. Urbee bikes, for example, must be brought back to the same station. You are allowed to return a Hello-Bike to any Hello-Bike station as the stations are clustered within the Zuidas area.

Alternatively, NS International, the international and intercity rail transport provider in the Netherlands, offers a bicycle rental service (the

Brightly coloured *OV-fiets* rental bikes, from NS International

OV-fiets) at its train stations (www.ns.nl/en/door-to-door/ov-fiets). Their bicycles are sturdy, heavy, and come equipped with pedal-powered lights, a rear-mounted rack, a wheel lock, a chain lock, and foot brakes.

To rent a bicycle from NS, you first need to have a public transport card that is linked to a Dutch bank account (also known as a personal *OV-chipkaart*). You may then apply for the *OV-fiets* service using your personal *OV-chipkaart*, for a token subscription rate of €0.01 per year. The *OV-fiets* is particularly convenient if you are commuting by train to another city, and want to rent a bicycle for the last leg of your journey. At large stations, there are often hundreds of bicycles available, stored in racks and manned by an attendant. At smaller stations, the number of bicycles may be limited, and sometimes there is no availability. You can check the number of bicycles that are present at a given location in advance, using the *OV-fiets* smart phone app. Each time you borrow an *OV-fiets*, a payment of around €4 is automatically deducted from your bank account. You can use the bicycle for the next 24 hours, after which you will have to pay an additional fee. You may rent up to two bicycles at any given time. Note that if you return your *OV-fiets* to a different location from the one at which you picked it up, you will be charged an additional fee of €10.

Bicycle maintenance

A bicycle requires regular maintenance in order to function reliably and smoothly. At a minimum, the tires should be pumped up correctly, the chain should be oiled, and the brakes should be working. To determine how hard your tires should be, check the manufacturer's specifications, which are printed on sides of the tires. These state the recommended range of air pressure that should be maintained inside the tires (the units are typically in pounds per square inch or bars). The optimum pressure will fall somewhere within this range, depending on your body weight. The more you (and your baggage) weigh, the higher the pressure should be.[14] When your tires start to lose air, your pedalling efficiency decreases and it takes more effort to cover the same distance.

If your tires become completely deflated, you should avoid riding on them or placing significant weight on the bicycle, as you risk damaging the rims of the wheels.

Foot pumps can be purchased from bicycle shops, and while they are cheap and easy to use, they are large and hence harder to carry around. Hand pumps are portable, but good-quality ones tend to be more expensive than foot pumps and may require more effort to use. Also take note that if you leave your pump with your parked bicycle, it might get stolen. Many businesses have employees who cycle to work and they keep a pump on the premises in case it is needed. If you need to pump up your tire urgently and you do not have a pump, you could pop into a shop, a café, or a restaurant, and ask the staff whether they have a pump that you can borrow. If the need arises, you could even consider knocking on doors to ask the inhabitants for assistance.

If you experience mechanical problems, such as with your brakes, chain, or gears, and do not want to fix them yourself, you can bring your bicycle to a shop for repair (there are 140 bicycle shops in Amsterdam alone).

Accessories

Bicycle lights and reflectors are mandatory (more details are provided below, in the section on 'Lights'). A bell allows you to warn others of your presence and give them time to respond to you. For more information on how to use the bell appropriately, refer to the section on 'Using the bell' in Chapter 3. To transport goods, people often use a pair of panniers, which are typically positioned on either side of the back or the front wheel, or a basket (sometimes consisting of a simple crate, attached to either the front or the back of the bike). Note that while a crate is cheap and spacious, its large size can make it cumbersome to park in a spot that is crammed full of other bikes. Similarly, it is harder for other cyclists to fit their bike into a parking space that is adjacent to one containing a bike with a crate.

A crate mounted over the front rack serves as a basket

A sturdy metal rack over your front or rear tire (known as a *bagage-drager*) can also be used to transport goods or a passenger. Large objects can be secured to the rack using rope or elastic bungee cords with hooks at either end (also known as luggage straps). To protect your clothes (and those of the cyclists behind you) when the roads are wet, it is helpful to install mudguards over the tires. For hands-free calls, listening to music, or navigating with GPS while cycling, people sometimes mount a phone holder to the handlebars.

When searching for your bike amongst a crowd of other bikes, it helps to have some unique identifying features to make it stand out. Some cyclists personalise their bicycle with spray paint, artificial plants and flowers, or even stuffed toys. Sometimes a colourful seat cover is used to protect the seat from rain, which simultaneously aids identification of the bicycle.

Be prepared to spend €30-50 on a good bicycle lock from a reputable vendor, such as a bicycle shop or a street market stall at Waterlooplein or Albert Cuypstraat. Do not compromise on quality – cheap locks may look identical to expensive ones, but they are made from low-quality metal that bike thieves can easily saw through. According to the *Fietsersbond* (the Dutch Cyclists' Union), the most effective solution is to use a wheel lock in combination with a chain lock that measures at least 85 cm in length, thus ensuring that you are able to lock your bicycle to something solid.[15] To keep your lock in optimal working condition, apply some mechanical oil (such as *onderhoudsspray* or 'maintenance spray') to the keyhole regularly. Otherwise, you may find that your lock gradually becomes stiff and eventually refuses to open up. For more information on how to park and lock up your bike, refer to the section on 'Parking, locks, and theft' in Chapter 3.

Lights

Bicycle lights are mandatory in the Netherlands, and attributes such as their location and beam colour have to comply with legal requirements. To ensure that you are maximally visible to other road users at night or when visibility is poor, ensure that you have reflectors on your pedals and wheels, as well as mounted bicycle lights (white or yellow headlights for the front of the bicycle, and red taillights for the rear). The lights should produce a constant beam and not be flashing. Bicycle lights may either be battery-powered or pedal-powered (for the latter, the lights only come on when you are pedalling, by means of a dynamo system). Adjust the position of your lights so that they do not point directly into the eyes of other road users and cause temporary blindness – instead, where possible, direct them at a slight angle downward, towards the ground.

As an alternative to mounted bicycle lights, you are also permitted to wear headlights on your chest and taillights on your back (such as LED lights on a keychain). To ensure that the lights remain continually visible in a stable position, wear them on your upper body and refrain from wearing them on your head, legs or arms. If you do not comply with these regulations and are caught, you will receive a fine.

Posture

Your posture will depend on the style of bicycle that you ride. A more crouched-over posture, such as that adopted by cyclists on road bikes, for example, makes it easier to pedal strongly but harder to see your surroundings. A more upright posture, such as that seen with an Amsterdam 'city bike', makes it easier to monitor what is going on around you.

When it comes to seat height, most guidelines state that the seat should be at approximately the same height as your hip when you are standing next to the bike, and that when you are seated in the saddle, your legs should be almost fully extended while cycling. This helps to reduce the strain on your knees, particularly if you are cycling for long periods of time. This also allows you to make use of your body weight when pedalling.

To understand why the guidelines recommend placing the seat at this height, think of cycling as being more akin to walking than to sitting. When you walk, you transfer your body weight from one leg

The typical, upright posture of a cyclist on an omafiets

to the other. Similarly, to maximise efficiency while cycling, your body weight should shift from one pedal to another. When your leg is extended, you should effectively be 'standing' on the pedal, and much of your body weight should be borne by your leg, rather than by the saddle.

If you follow these recommendations, your toes may barely touch the ground when you are seated in the saddle, requiring you to jump down from the saddle, or to place a foot on the curb when you come to a stop.

For cyclists who are just starting to learn the rules of the road and are concentrating on getting around safely, it might feel dangerous or frightening to place the saddle at the height that is considered 'maximally efficient' for cycling.

While waiting, cyclists jump down from their seat or place a foot on the curb

My recommendation is to take things one step at a time, and to not feel pressured to do something you're not ready for. If you like being able to place your feet on the ground while you are seated in the saddle, in the event that you need to brake suddenly, then by all means adjust the seat so that you feel comfortable. As you grow familiar with the road and the behaviour of other users, you can always raise your seat accordingly.

Further reading

For a comprehensive range of information on cycling in the Netherlands, an organisation known as the *Fietsersbond* (the Dutch Cyclists' Union) provides extensive information and tips on their website (in Dutch):

- www.fietsersbond.nl/de-fiets/

The following websites offer more information (in Dutch) on the types of locks available, with tips on how to lock up your bicycle:

- www.fietsersbond.nl
- www.beewise.nl

ROAD SIGNS

CHAPTER 2

Cycle lanes

Cycle lanes may be indicated by one or more of the following signs: A symbol of a bicycle that is painted on the ground inside the lane. A circular blue sign containing a white symbol of a bicycle, which indicates a mandatory cycle path (e.g. G12a). And a blue sign with the word *fietspad* ('cycle path') in white lettering, which indicates an optional cycle path (G13).

A cycle path

Sign G12a: A mandatory cycle path for bicycles and mopeds

Sign G11: A mandatory cycle path. Note how cyclists keep to the right

Sign G13: An optional cycle path

Sign G14 (bottom): End of the optional cycle path

Technically, if a bicycle lane is demarcated by a solid line, then other vehicles are not allowed to enter into it. Be well aware that in practice, drivers often break the rules, and the bicycle lane does not guarantee protection – you must keep a constant lookout for danger and warning signs. If the bicycle lane is marked by a broken line, then other vehicles are allowed to use it as a right-turn lane, meaning that they may enter the bicycle lane if they are planning to turn right at a junction. As with other vehicular traffic, bicycles are required to keep to the right of the cycle lane.

A 'recommended' cycle lane

'Recommended' cycle lanes

On some roads, a lane is marked by a broken line but does not contain symbols of a bicycle. This indicates a 'recommended' cycle lane, meaning that cars are allowed to stop on it, if it is safe for them to do so.

Exceptions

In many cases, cyclists are exempted from the rule that is depicted on a sign. This exemption is indicated by an extra sign (known as a 'supplementary road sign') underneath the first, containing the word *uitgezonderd* (meaning 'except for'), followed by one or more symbols of vehicles. This means that the rule applies to all types of vehicles, except the ones depicted on the *uitgezonderd* sign.

The arrow indicates a one-way road, but bicycles and mopeds are exempted from this rule

All vehicles, except for bicycles, are
required to turn right at this junction

This 'no access' sign does not
apply to cyclists

Sign E3: Parking of bicycles and
mopeds is prohibited

Access and parking signs

A sign that contains a symbol of a bicycle within a red circle (C14) indicates that you are forbidden from cycling on that road.

A sign that contains a symbol of a bicycle against a blue background (G11 and G12a) indicates that bicycles are required to use that road or path. A sign that contains a symbol of a bicycle on a blue background with a red slash across it (G12) indicates the end of a bicycle route.

A sign of a bicycle on a blue background within a red circle and with a red slash across it (E3) indicates that bicycles are not allowed to park at that spot.

Sign C14:
No access for bicycles

Sign G12: End of the cycle path.
Below it: 'Watch out for the tram!'

This sign warns road users to stop and pay attention

Warning signs

Warning signs caution road users to pay special attention to their surroundings. A symbol of a red upside-down triangle signals that you should stop and check that the way is clear, before continuing. A sign stating *Pas op!* means, 'Watch out!' Sometimes you may encounter obstacles, such as speed bumps (*drempels*), or cattle grids (*rooster*). The sign *Slecht wegdek* means 'bad road'.

One-way roads

One-way roads are marked by a sign containing a white arrow against a blue square. Bicycles are often exempted from this rule. For example, if the symbol of a bicycle is present on the supplementary *uitgezonderd* sign, then the road is one-way for cars, but remains two-way for cyclists.

Direction signposts

Signposts for cyclists indicate the distance in kilometres to surrounding destinations, and have red lettering against a white background (K7 and K8). If there is more than one route to a destination, as occasionally happens, then the alternative route is indicated in green lettering. Generally speaking, the route indicated by red lettering is the more direct one, whereas that marked by green lettering is a scenic/recreational route.

Sign K7/K8: A direction signpost outside the Vondelpark

Cycling is allowed in these pedestrian zones

Pedestrian areas

Pedestrian areas are indicated by a rectangular sign with symbols of pedestrians against a blue circular background. If there is an additional sign underneath, with the words *fietsers toegestaan*, or the word *toegestaan* together with a symbol of a bicycle, then cycling is permitted within the pedestrian zone.

This exemption for bicycles may also depend on the time of year and/or day. A network of streets in the city centre, including the popular shopping streets of Kalverstraat and Nieuwendijk, and the streets adjacent to them, are pedestrian-only zones, and cycling is not permitted. If you want to traverse this area, then you need to walk your bicycle.

Further reading

The Dutch Ministry of Transport publishes a useful and detailed guidebook, 'Road Traffic Signs and Regulations in the Netherlands', which is an abridged version of '1990 Traffic Rules and Signs Regulations' (RVV 1990) and is available for download here:[16]
- www.rijksoverheid.nl

The full version, '1990 Traffic Rules and Signs Regulations' (RVV 1990), is in Dutch and can be accessed online here:
- http://wetten.overheid.nl/BWBR0004825/2017-01-01

More information in Dutch, including a list of FAQs for cyclists, can be found on the website of the Government of the Netherlands:[17]
- www.rijksoverheid.nl/onderwerpen/fiets

An unofficial compilation of some of the road signs that are most relevant to cyclists can be found on the blog, 'Bicycle Dutch':[18]
- https://bicycledutch.wordpress.com

TIPS AND ETIQUETTE FOR CYCLISTS

CHAPTER 3

Aside from the mandatory regulations accompanying the road signs in the previous chapter, there are many other rules that govern cyclists' behaviour, some of which are unwritten. Certain rules should be strictly adhered to in the vast majority of cases, whereas other rules or guidelines can be heeded or ignored, depending on the situation. As a beginner, you may occasionally feel perplexed when you observe other people breaking a rule that you have just committed to memory – or abashed when other people reprimand you for breaking a rule.

Truth be told, in the real world, all rules get broken at some point in time. Experienced cyclists know how to gauge their situation and behave in a way that conforms to the expectations of their fellow road users – whether that is in keeping with the 'hard and fast' rules, or goes somewhat against them. Acquisition of this knowledge requires a combination of practice and trial and error; this chapter aims to speed up the learning process by describing what is expected of you, the rationale behind it, and the degree to which it is expected.

The 'rule of the road'

In the Netherlands, in keeping with the rest of continental Europe, the direction of traffic flow is on the right. Hence, in the vast majority of cases, you will be cycling on the right side of the road. Exceptions to this rule may occur, for instance, when the bicycle lane is shifted

towards the middle or the left of the street, or when there is a traffic diversion and you are rerouted towards the left.

Looking around and making eye contact

As a cyclist, you are one of many users on the road. Situational awareness is crucial, and you need to constantly look around and assess your surroundings. If you are on a converging path with another road user, look in their direction to indicate that you have seen them. If a car is about to cross paths with you and you have the right of way, never assume that they have seen you – slow down and make sure that they have spotted you, and come to a stop if necessary. Feel free to look all the way over your shoulder and make obvious movements with your head and torso. If you are leery of making eye contact with strangers or are concerned about

One of the rare cases in which the cycle lane shifts to the left side of the road

looking vulnerable, rest assured that Amsterdam is considered to be a very safe city, with lower rates of street harassment than cities such as New York or San Francisco. A benefit of being on a bike is that if you encounter street harassers and they are on foot, you can move past or get away from them relatively quickly.

Using the bell

As with car horns, the bicycle bell should be used only when necessary, to alert people to your presence and intentions, and not to scold, reprimand, or harass them. Adjust how vigorously and loudly you ring your bell to the situation – along a quiet street with few people, a gentle ring is usually enough, whereas a busy street with high levels of traffic may require several strong rings. Alternatively, you may call out a warning or ask people to make way for you. Keep in mind that tourists may not be used to bicycles or appreciate having bells rung at them. It helps to remain calm and anticipate that their reactions may vary from being apologetic and jumping out of the way, to being reluctant to move or even becoming aggressive and verbally abusive. Be courteous and thank people if they make way for you, while ignoring those who behave badly (refer to the section on 'Bad behaviour' in Chapter 3, for more information about dealing with untoward behaviour). If you startle someone or come close to colliding with them, a simple apology can go a long way.

Visibility

As far as possible, ensure that you have a clear, wide view of the road, and use your peripheral vision to detect hazards and approaching objects while they are still at a distance. On occasion, this may be difficult – if you are wearing a jacket or hoodie that restricts your vision; if a vehicle or building is blocking your view; if it is foggy, raining or snowing; or if the wind blows hair across your eyes. Before your ride, try to prepare yourself by wearing clothing that is appropriate to your commute. If needed, wear a hat or a jacket that shields your eyes from rain and glare, and use a hair band or a hair tie to secure your hair. If the sun shines directly into your eyes, this can impair your vision. Similarly, when a driver is approaching from the opposite direction and the sun is shining directly into their eyes, remember that they may not be able to see you clearly or at all.

At night, when cycling in poorly lit areas, car headlights can be blinding. Headlights are typically angled downwards towards the ground, but if nearby vehicles are travelling along a road that is slightly elevated relative to the cycle path, or going over a bridge, this may cause the lights to shine directly into your eyes. If your bicycle lights are on, illuminating your surroundings, this problem can be alleviated. If you can barely see, it may be safer to slow down or stop and wait until the glare is reduced, or to follow the lead of other cyclists. More information on bicycle lights can be found in the section on 'Lights' in Chapter 1.

Traffic lights

There are several sets of traffic lights in the city of Amsterdam – one for fast-moving vehicles such as cars and motorcycles, one for pedestrians, and one for cyclists (and sometimes mopeds and scooters as well). The traffic lights for cyclists contain the symbol of a bicycle, and there are typically two sets of lights at each crossing; one set is positioned at approximately eye level, for cyclists who are waiting directly in front of the traffic light, and one set is positioned higher up, for the cyclists who are waiting further behind.

These traffic lights have a third set of indicator lights, for turning right

Some traffic lights are accompanied by
countdown timers, which display the number of
seconds left until a red light turns green. The display
stops updating when the timer reaches a certain
number of seconds (typically 5 seconds), hence the
display remains frozen on the same number for
several seconds, after which the lights turn green.
It is not uncommon for locals to carry on the countdown in their head, check whether the coast is clear,
and start crossing the road even before the traffic
light turns green. Some junctions do not have dedicated traffic lights for cyclists. In these cases, cyclists
follow the same traffic lights as the cars.

When the light turns green in your favour,
make sure to check that no vehicles are approaching
before you cross the road. Drivers do occasionally run
red lights or try to get through at the last second.
Similarly, other cyclists or motorcyclists may run red
lights or attempt to squeeze through, cutting in front
of you. It is usually best to be patient and let them
pass by quickly. Be especially careful to check for cars
that are located to your left and are waiting to turn
right – sometimes the light for these cars turns green
at the same time as the light for the cyclists. This tells
the car drivers that they are allowed to make a right
turn *if* the coast is clear and there are no cyclists
crossing the road. However, car drivers who are
unfamiliar with the local rules and roads may not

realise that they are supposed to wait for cyclists, and accelerate into the cycle lane instead.

If you are turning right at a traffic light with the sign *Rechtsaf voor fietsers vrij* ('right turn allowed for cyclists'), you are permitted to turn right even if the light is red, as long as the way is clear. At these junctions, there may already be cyclists occupying the cycle lane, waiting for the light to change so that they can cross the road. If there is room, you may be able to cycle past them and turn right, while keeping an eye on the traffic light to ensure that you do not get caught in their path when they start to move again. If the way is blocked, you may prefer to wait with them in the cycle lane for the light to turn green, before turning right.

At tram and rail crossings, flashing white lights indicate that you can cross, while flashing red lights signal that you need to stop.

Signals at a train crossing with no barriers

Turning left at a traffic light in one stage

At some traffic lights, a designated area for cyclists is located in front of the stopped cars. Cyclists can occupy this box while waiting, and then move ahead in front of the cars while turning left on the green light.

Turning left at a traffic light in two stages

At the majority of traffic junctions, cyclists need to make a left turn in two stages; they cross the first road and wait at the corner, and then they cross the second road, which is perpendicular to the first. Some traffic junctions have a dedicated 'waiting area' for cyclists who are in

The cyclist stops in a special buffer zone while waiting for the second light to turn green

Cyclists may wait in the red box in front of the cars

between crossings, and the waiting area is equipped with its own traffic light. This is particularly true if the junction tends to be busy and cyclists regularly need to turn left.

Other traffic junctions lack such a 'waiting area'. Sometimes, after crossing the first road, the cyclist is not able to enter the cycle lane and is positioned too far in front of the traffic light to see when it changes. In these situations, cyclists have to use their common sense, squeezing into whatever space is available, and waiting for cues from other road users or the cyclists behind them to know when to cross. If it seems very difficult to cross or to detect when the traffic light changes in your favour, you can always get off your bicycle and either wheel it back to the start of the cycle lane, or cross the road as a pedestrian, following the pedestrian lights.

Following pedestrian lights

Typically, when crossing a multilane road, the traffic lights for cyclists are configured to take the average cycling speed into account, hence their signals may differ from those for the pedestrians.

For example, pedestrians are often able to cross the road lane by lane, whereas cyclists may only be given the go-ahead when several consecutive lanes are clear. It is quite common to see cyclists who ignore the traffic light for cyclists, and cross the road in a similar manner to that of pedestrians, either checking one lane at a time to see if it is clear and 'jay-walking', or following the pedestrian traffic lights. In theory, one would imagine that if pedestrians have a green light, then it should also be perfectly safe for cyclists to cross. Keep in mind, however, that in these situations, other road users (such as approaching cars and cyclists) may be looking out specifically for pedestrians, and adjust their behaviour to take the presence and speed of pedestrians into account, but not that of faster-moving cyclists. Hence, other drivers may not give you sufficient time or clearance to cross the road. If you engage in unexpected behaviour, make sure to take extra precautions and check your surroundings carefully.

Zebra crossings

Cyclists and vehicles are supposed to stop for pedestrians at zebra crossings. In practice, however, this rule is not strictly followed in Amsterdam, for various reasons. If cyclists are moving at speed, it can be difficult for them to stop in time for pedestrians. If they brake abruptly, this may cause cyclists who are close behind to collide with them. This is especially true if one encounters a zebra crossing immediately after having gone through a traffic light. If the cyclists in front slow down or stop, this could cause the cyclists behind them to 'pile up' on the road, directly in front of cars that are about to start moving. Fast-moving cyclists often assume that pedestrians will discern that it is easier for pedestrians to stop than it is for cyclists to stop, and that they will wait patiently for the cyclist to pass.

On some roads, each lane has its own set of traffic lights

In reality, this may or may not happen – pedestrians who are used to giving way to cyclists or who are cyclists themselves may indeed wait for the cyclist to pass. However, in many cities and countries around the world, zebra crossings are revered and it is unusual or even shocking when cars and vehicles fail to yield to pedestrians. If pedestrians expect cyclists to stick to the rules, they may not even think of checking the road at a zebra crossing, let alone yield to a cyclist. Hence, cyclists may need to quickly give way, by braking abruptly or cycling onto the pavement or the car lane to circumvent the pedestrians. As a cyclist, the safest strategy is to slow down when approaching a zebra cross-ing with pedestrians, in anticipation that they may attempt to cross. If there is already a steady stream of cyclists

moving across the zebra crossing, or the pedestrians are clearly holding back, and waiting for you to pass, then it is fine to pass through with a smile of thanks.

Priority road markings

Smaller junctions and crossings may not be equipped with traffic lights. Instead, one has to rely on priority road markings in the form of isosceles triangles (also known as 'shark's teeth' due to their triangular shape, or *haaientanden* in Dutch) that are painted on the road.

If the points of the 'teeth' are facing you, you need to give way. If there are no shark's teeth on your lane, and there are shark's teeth

Pedestrians wait patiently at a zebra crossing for the stream of cyclists to pass

The shark's teeth indicate that the cyclists have priority over the car

pointed towards someone in another lane, then you have the right of way and they are supposed to yield to you. As always, keep in mind that not all road users follow the rules, and sometimes people may not yield to you even if you have the right of way, particularly if they are going fast and feel that it is difficult for them to slow down in time. Where possible, play it safe by making eye contact and by adjusting your speed so that you can brake if necessary.

'Keep clear' road markings

At an intersection, a box painted on the ground, containing diagonal lines in the form of a cross, indicates that this region is to be kept clear of traffic and you are not supposed to stop inside the box. When stopping for a red traffic light, for example, you need to make sure that

Keep the space within the box free for passing traffic

there is sufficient room for others to cross the path that you are on. If there is not enough room beyond the 'keep clear' markings, then you need to stop before the box.

Flashing yellow lights

At certain intersections or times of the day with low levels of traffic, traffic lights are not installed. Instead, these intersections are equipped with flashing yellow lights, which tell road users to proceed with caution and go ahead if the coast is clear. Be ready to slow down or stop when crossing, and stay alert!

Cyclists wait for cars to pass, at a set of flashing yellow lights

Signalling

If you behave in a predictable manner and indicate your intentions, other road users will have more time to adjust their own behaviour. Hence, as long as there are other road users around, it is both important and courteous to signal whenever you are about to stop, slow down or turn a corner. If you are about to come to a stop and dismount your bicycle, use one hand to indicate the side on which you will be stopping.

Before sticking your hand out, check to make sure that you do not hit someone with it. If possible, exit the bicycle lane and dismount on the pavement, so as to stay out of the way of other cyclists. When turning, whether at a traffic light, a junction, or a fork in the road, indicate the

direction that you will be taking. This allows other cyclists to adjust their speed accordingly – if they are behind you, they might slow down while keeping behind you, or move to overtake you. If they are approaching from a different direction, your gesture will let them know whether they are about to cross paths with you, or whether they can move past without crossing. This will allow them to decide whether to slow down, or to continue at the same speed.

Signal your intentions when turning or stopping

You will occasionally notice it when other cyclists fail to signal, even though they are slowing down, stopping, or turning directly in front of you. This is especially annoying when they do so abruptly and you are moving fast or are in the process of overtaking them. Sometimes, you may notice them turning their head slightly to check for traffic, or they may slow down or stop pedalling. Remember that people's actions are often unpredictable, and that it is courteous to give others advance notice of your intentions.

Choosing 'sides' within the cycle lane and overtaking

Although you should generally keep close to the right side of the cycle lane, on occasion you may need to move to the left side. For example, you may need to overtake someone, or prepare to turn to the left. By convention, overtaking is done on the left, and it is rarely advisable to overtake someone on their right as they are unlikely to be expecting it, particularly if there is limited space. Ensure that there is indeed enough room for you to pass on the left. Most cycle lanes permit two cyclists to pass each other in the same direction, but some are too narrow for this. If the other cyclist has room to move further to the right and make space for you, you can ring your bell to indicate that you would like to pass. Give the other cyclist as much room as possible while overtaking, and go at a speed that neither startles nor endangers them. Once you have passed safely, move to the right of the cycle lane again.

Alternatively, you may be preparing to turn to the left – whether at a traffic light, or at an intersection. If this is the case, you should indicate your intentions as soon as possible and prepare for the upcoming turn. Check whether there is anyone approaching from behind or to your left. Position yourself and move towards the left side of the cycle lane, taking care to signal with your left hand and using your body language, such as

A cyclist waits at the road
divider for cars to pass

slowing down and making eye contact. Conversely, if another cyclist moves to the left side of the cycle lane and signals their intention to turn left, then you can overtake them on the right.

Cutting across a lane for oncoming traffic

If you need to cut across a lane of oncoming traffic in order to turn into a road that does not have a traffic light, you have several options to choose from. If the traffic flow is light, you might be able to wait for a pause in traffic, or turn straight away. If there is a road divider and there is enough space, you may be able to wait in the middle of the road. Alternatively, you could wait until the coast is clear in all directions. If the traffic is heavy, you might be better off cycling to the nearest traffic light or zebra crossing, and cross there. Regardless, remember to signal your intentions and pay close attention to your surroundings.

Sometimes, the bicycle lane has a designated exit to the left, allowing you to keep out of the way of other cyclists while waiting for a break in the traffic. This is often the case when there is a road divider or a raised kerb between the cycle lane and the car lanes. Remember to signal as you move to the left of the cycle lane.

Staying close to the curb

Traffic regulations advise cyclists to stay as close to the right of the bicycle lane as possible, as this puts more distance between yourself and the cars, and also gives other cyclists and motorcyclists room to overtake you. For cyclists who are used to having the whole road to themselves, this may take some practice. At the beginning, if you are not used to cycling along a smooth, narrow trajectory, you may be afraid of either veering off into traffic or hitting a pedal against the raised curb. Hugging the curb requires a combination of motor control, balance, and practice, and develops over time. However, it is an extremely useful skill to have, as it allows you to take up less space and reduces your chances of colliding with other road users or objects. Depending on the circumstances, cyclists sometimes deviate from this rule – they may move towards the left of the cycle lane in order to avoid a pot hole, a bump, a manhole cover, a puddle, tree roots, glass, drips from overhead, another road user, and so on.

Cycling next to parked cars

Sometimes, a lane of parking spots for cars is positioned either to the right or to the left of the cycle lane. Regardless of the side on which they are located, keep a lookout for cars that are just about to enter or exit the parking lane. They will typically have their lights on and have their wheels pointed at an angle to the dividing line. If a vehicle blocks your way while it waits to turn into a parking spot, look over your shoulder to check whether there is traffic behind you, in the form of motorised vehicles or other cyclists. If all is clear, you can move alongside the waiting vehicle and overtake it. If there is too much traffic behind you and there is no room to overtake the waiting vehicle, you may need to stop behind it and wait.

When passing a vehicle that is in the process of pulling out of a parking spot, make sure that the driver can see you, and give it as much room as necessary. This way, if the vehicle pulls out suddenly or at high speed, you will be able to avoid it in time. Similarly, if a parked vehicle contains occupants, make sure that you are not going too fast or too close to the vehicle, as a door may open unexpectedly.

Cycling two or more abreast

According to traffic regulations, no more than two people are allowed to cycle side-by-side with each other (except when overtaking), but in practice, people often cycle three-or-more-abreast, particularly when travelling together with friends.

If you see a group of cyclists occupying most of the bicycle path (typically school children, but also teenagers and adults), heading towards you, do not panic. If they are locals and experienced road users, they will most likely merge smoothly into their own lane and make way for you – although also note that this may take place at the last second. If they come too close for comfort, stay calm and remember that they are used to cycling in close proximity with others, hence their concept of what constitutes a safe distance may be much smaller than yours. If they are tourists, however, then it is wise to slow down and anticipate having to stop or navigate around them. If you need to overtake a group of people, you can ring the bell to let them know that you want to pass. Those on the left will either slow down or speed up, and move to the right, making way for you. If you are cycling with friends and occupying more than one bicycle width, be sure to make way for other road users who need to overtake you.

Cycling in the opposite direction

Generally speaking, cyclists usually cycle on the right side of the road, following the rest of vehicular traffic. For various reasons, people sometimes end up cycling on the left side of the road instead – for exam-

ple, they may need to make a left-hand turn into an upcoming road, or would like to reach a destination on the 'wrong' side of the road. They may prefer to go along the 'wrong' side of the road than to go out of their way to cross at an official junction. Whatever it is, when people come towards you along the same bicycle lane, try to accommodate them by keeping to the right while they pass on the left. If there is not enough space for both of you, it would be courteous for them to slow down, move to the pavement, or stop, giving you a clear passage. Anticipate that this may not always happen and be prepared to slow down to avoid a collision if necessary.

Making tight turns

Dutch roads are designed with the needs of cyclists in mind. For example, attention is paid to the safety of the cyclist, the turning radius required for cyclists to make a smooth turn at high speed, and the flow of traffic. Nevertheless, you will occasionally encounter sharp corners with limited visibility, and busy intersections with winding cycle paths. You may come across stretches of cycle lane that are S-shaped, where cyclists need to make one quick turn after another, in opposite directions. Sometimes the gradient of the road changes rapidly, such as when going over a bridge or through an underpass or an overpass, and a tight turn is required.

At first, sharp turns may seem daunting – while other cyclists speed by effortlessly, you worry about losing your balance and falling off. Furthermore, it is often necessary to signal your intention to turn, meaning that you will only have one hand on the handlebar while you signal and turn. If you plan far enough in advance before the turn, you may be able to signal quickly with one hand, and then go back to using both hands to steer. However, your ultimate goal should be to master the ability to turn while signalling.

Making a tight turn through an underpass

There is more to navigating a turn than simply using your arms to steer the handlebar. You need to maintain forward momentum while leaning into the turn with your whole body, which will allow you to make turns at a sharper angle. The danger is that if you lean too much or too little, or your tire slips or hits an obstacle, you may lose control or tip over. Hence, you should go at a reasonable speed (neither too fast nor too slow) and only lean as much as necessary, ensuring that your path is free of obstacles, such as raised curbs or road dividers, or slippery patches, such as refuse or fallen leaves. A useful technique is to look not only at the path immediately in front you (while scanning for obstacles), but to also direct your gaze at the part of the path that lies beyond the turn. This automatically shifts your body weight and posture in the direction that you are aiming for, and helps you to lean into the turn. The grip of your tires will also determine how safe it is to lean at a sharp angle – generally speaking, larger treads with deep grooves provide more grip than smooth tires with shallow grooves, but this also depends on the quality and make of the tires.

To avoid scraping your pedal or your foot against the ground when you lean, pause your pedalling during the turn, and keep the inner pedal at the maximum height from the ground.

Speeds and gears

Although the Netherlands is one of the flattest countries in the world, in terms of its large-scale geography, the city of Amsterdam has numerous bridges over its canals and a fair number of underpasses and overpasses, some of which can be quite steep. It can also be rather windy, with average wind speeds of over 11 knots, and strong, buffeting gusts that are several times the average. For more information about wind conditions in the Netherlands, refer to the section on 'Wind' in Chapter 5.

The wind is also known as 'the Dutch hill', because cycling against or with the wind is akin to cycling up or down a hill. The amount of effort it takes to pedal is dependent on the gradient of the land and the strength of the wind. Accordingly, you may find it necessary to switch gears to adjust the amount of effort required for each rotation of the pedals. To expend less effort, switch to a lower gear (i.e. shift the chain so that it wraps around a smaller cog). The distance covered per rotation of the pedals decreases, but each rotation is easier to execute. To speed up or to take advantage of a downward gradient, you can switch to a higher gear. The speed of cyclists in Amsterdam varies substantially, depending on the bicycle and the rider, but on average, the pace is modest, at approximately 14.4 km/h.[19] Select a gear that is appropriate for you and does not place excessive force on your knee joints. Cycling for long periods at too high a gear can lead to injury – if your knees are hurting, try shifting to a lower gear and/or adjusting the height of your seat.

Slowing down and braking

When cycling in a city environment, you need to continually adjust your speed to suit the circumstances. At a minimum, you need to be able to stop abruptly, and adjust your position and distance to other road users. Ideally, you want to be able to slow down, stop, and speed up at a moment's notice, and this requires practice and good balance. After stopping or slowing down, you often need to take up speed again, which is easiest if you have not already come to a complete stop. Maintaining your balance while moving forwards very slowly, or not at all, is hence an extremely useful skill, as it allows you to move at a snail's pace, and yet accelerate rapidly when needed. If you anticipate having to stop at a traffic light or slow down for another road user, for example, it may be sufficient to cease pedalling, to pedal more slowly, or to brake only lightly. You may stand on the pedals, adjusting the position of your body for finer control over your balance, and buying some extra time while you wait. A standing position also allows you to use your body weight to exert more downward force on the pedals, such as when accelerating or going up a hill. Furthermore, if you are accustomed to getting out of your saddle and standing on the ground when you come to a stop, then standing on the pedals is an intermediate step to doing so.

When you brake or slow down, try to indicate your intentions to the road users behind you. You can do this by signalling with your hand, turning your head to check whether someone is close behind you, and/or ceasing to pedal. If you are braking abruptly to avoid a serious collision, e.g. with a motorised vehicle, you may not have any time to signal. It is hence advisable to leave sufficient distance between you and the cyclist in front of you, in case the other person needs to slow down abruptly. The higher your speed, the more distance is required to decelerate.

If your bicycle has a pair of hand brakes, it can be helpful to check and remember which hand controls the back wheel, and which the front, especially if you need to decelerate abruptly or cycle in wet, slippery conditions. If you are moving at high speed and brake hard using only your front brake, there is a risk that your rear wheel may lift off the ground while your front wheel stays locked, sending you flying over your handlebars. This is particularly true when cycling steeply downhill. Similarly, if you are on a slippery surface and brake using only your front brake, your front wheel may lose traction and slip. Under such circumstances, it may be wise to engage primarily the rear brake.

Hand brakes are controlled via cables that run along the exterior of the bicycle frame. If the brakes stop working, it may be because the cables are bent (in which case you can simply straighten the cables), or broken. At freezing-cold temperatures, ice may form around the cables, preventing them from functioning normally (for more information, refer to the section on 'Snow and ice' in Chapter 5).

If your bicycle has foot brakes, then the pedals cannot be spun backwards freely, as described in the section on 'Brakes' in Chapter 1. Hence, when coming to a stop (such as at a traffic light), you should position the pedals such that one of them is at its maximum height. This will allow you to step down upon it with the maximum momentum, in order to gain speed when it is time to take off again. If you are not used to foot brakes, it will take some practice to learn how to apply the right amount of braking

pressure in a smooth, controlled manner, using your feet. Also note that if you get out of your seat and stand on the pedals, any backwards pressure on your pedals will cause you to brake. Hence, you need to position your pedals such that you are able to keep your balance, and apply the brake only when desired.

Distractions

Sometimes, you may be so absorbed by something in your surroundings (such as the actions of another road user), that you are temporarily unable to pay attention to other events. This is normal, especially when you are starting out and every step requires your full concentration. Nonetheless, your eventual goal should be to distribute your attention optimally, focusing on one or two key events while still scanning the other aspects of your environment.

Choices and conflicting actions

Occasionally, you are presented with a choice between two conflicting actions – for example, to either slow down or speed up. If you are confident that you have the right of way and that other road users have seen you and are reacting accordingly, you may feel free to carry on without adjusting your behaviour. If you are unsure, do not have the right of way, or are concerned about the safety of yourself or others, be especially prepared to adjust your behaviour as needed. You may sometimes need to carry out two rather different actions in rapid succession – for example, speeding up to overtake someone or cross a road, and then stopping abruptly to accommodate someone else. Often, you can avoid such situations simply by looking ahead, spotting potential traffic snarls, and slowing down, giving way, or adjusting your behaviour in anticipation of obstacles.

Road works, diversions, and obstacles

The city is a dynamic environment. Even when cycling along a familiar route, you may be faced with road works, repairs, or unexpected obstacles. Sometimes you will encounter road diversions (*omleiding*), in which sections of road are blocked off for maintenance or construction work. Small changes may be hard to detect in advance, especially if your view is obstructed by other cyclists and road users. Major changes are generally marked by signs, orange cones, or fencing, and there may be a worker stationed at the diversion to direct traffic. The word *volg*, meaning 'follow', instructs cyclists to follow the yellow signs containing a symbol of a bicycle. A sign such as *werkverkeer op pad* may be displayed, warning you that construction or maintenance vehicles, such as heavy-duty trucks and excavators, are in operation.

Follow the directions of the traffic officer and/or signage, and observe the behaviour of other cyclists. If the directions of the officer are in conflict with the signs, the officer's instructions take precedence. Sometimes planks are laid on the ground, forming a makeshift road, bridge, or ramp. If a large stretch of cycle lane is obstructed, this may necessitate a significant diversion to get to your destination, depending on the routes available. Sometimes temporary road markings (usually yellow) are painted onto the road. If present, they take precedence over the white lines.

Various types of barriers are used to regulate the flow of traffic. A chicane-style barrier consists of one or more staggered metal barriers that project into the cycle path, inhibiting the speed of cyclists and/or discouraging mopeds and scooters from entering. These are typically found at the beginning of a pedestrian zone or at areas where cyclists tend to go too fast, such as at the entrance to a steeply inclined underpass. Bollards are pole-like barriers that project out from the ground and are located on and along roads and cycle paths (also known as *paaltjes*). They are often placed at junctions between a cycle path and a road, to prevent cars from using the cycle path for an illegal shortcut or U-turn. A row of bollards between

Temporary road markings

Road works and diversions are typically marked by barriers and signs the road and the cycle path also helps to shield cyclists from auto-mobile traffic. Most bollards are painted in conspicuous or contrast-ing colours to enhance their visibil-ity. However, they also tend to be short, ending at or below waist level. Hence, it can be difficult to spot them, especially if you are cycling behind or amidst a group of people who obscure the path ahead. If, for example, you are attempting to overtake other cyclists along an unfamiliar stretch of road, you may unexpectedly encounter a bollard in the middle of the lane.

During rush hour, at busy intersections, you may encounter grid-locked traffic, with vehicles blocking your passage. If it is possible to find a way through the traffic, go slowly and carefully, watching the other vehicles closely. You may be able to follow the lead of other cyclists and moped riders as they carve a route through the traffic. Be prepared to use your bell, shout, stop abruptly, or even jump off your bike, if impatient or careless drivers make dangerous movements towards you or others. For more information, refer to the section on 'Blocked bicycle lanes' in Chapter 4.

Bridges

Some of the larger bridges over the canals of Amsterdam can be raised, to allow boats to pass through. If the traffic light is red (either constant or flashing), you must stop. Before the bridge opens, a warning signal is given, and traffic barriers are lowered to prevent vehicles from driving onto the bridge. Road users line up behind the barriers and wait for the bridge to reopen to traffic. Sometimes, if there are alternative options nearby or the bridge opening is likely to take a long time, cyclists may decide to take a different route.

Cyclists wait behind the barriers while a bridge closes

Gridlocked traffic

Parking, locks, and theft

There are approximately 250,000 parking spaces for bicycles in Amsterdam, the majority of which are located in public spaces. Bicycles may be parked on pavements, footpaths, at the roadside, and anywhere an official sign permits it.

At train stations throughout the city, there are places for approximately 26,000 bicycles in total (the area around Amsterdam Central Station alone has 10,000 bicycle parking spots)[20], while its metro and bus stations can accommodate approximately 7,000 bicycles in total. In addition, residential areas provide approximately 5,000 spots.[3]

Some bicycle parking garages are monitored 24/7 by a security guard, providing an extra level of protection.[21] This is particularly useful if your bicycle is expensive, or if you intend to leave it parked for an extended period of time. The Amsterdam City Council provides guarded bicycle parking garages at numerous locations in the city centre, including Stationseiland (next to Central Station), the Amstel, Sloterdijk, RAI, and Zuid stations, Nieuwmarkt, Rokin, Leideseplein, and Waterlooplein (www.amsterdam.nl/parkeren-verkeer/fiets/fietsparkeren/).[22] Parking is free-of-charge for the first 24 hours, after which a fee is levied. Depending on the precise location, bicycles may be left for a maximum of 2 to 6 weeks.

A range of private companies also offers guarded parking facilities, for various types of bicycles, scooters,

Bicycles may be parked in the designated areas for up to 14 days

The massive, multi-storey bicycle garage next to Central Station

mopeds, and motorcycles, and some may even accommodate other large objects such as prams and surfboards. A database of these services is provided by the website Stalling Amsterdam (www.stallingamsterdam.nl, in Dutch).[23]

Occasionally, signs explicitly forbid cyclists from parking in certain spots, such as the signs *Fietsen worden verwijderd*, which means 'bicycles will be removed', or *Verboden fietsen te plaatsen*, which means 'parking of bicycles is forbidden'.

In practice, you will see bicycles parked all over the place. Generally speaking, people often park their bikes wherever they can find a plausible spot – next to a lamppost, against bridge railings, next to buildings, and along the pavement. There are few hard and fast rules, but here are a few guidelines to keep in mind when selecting your parking spot: Make sure not to obstruct the passage of traffic. Do not park your bicycle in a cycle lane, or on a road – not only is your bicycle obstructing traffic, it could also get damaged or run over. Finally, try not to obstruct the exit routes of other parked vehicles. Sometimes, if an area is particularly crowded (if, for example, there is a well-attended event nearby, and there are bikes jammed into every corner), this is unavoidable. On such occasions, when retrieving your bicycle, you may end up having to extricate it slowly and carefully from a precariously-balanced crowd of bicycles.

Also be aware that in the crowded centre, it is quite common for bicycles to experience damage or wear and tear. For example, another vehicle or road user might crash into your bicycle while you are gone, leaving dents and scratches. Strong winds may knock your bicycle or adjacent bicycles over, causing a domino effect. If your bicycle falls into a bicycle lane or a road, it becomes vulnerable to traffic. Bicycles may shift position slightly, particularly if they are in a crowded spot, and other cyclists may move your bike slightly in order to park or retrieve theirs. Similarly, if your bicycle is parked outside an establishment such as a restaurant and the owner does not want to have bicycles cluttering the entrance, then they might move your bike to a less offensive spot.

Sign for a guarded bicycle
parking facility

Parking of bicycles is not allowed

Parking of bicycles, scooters, and motorcycles is not allowed

Any parked bicycles
will be removed by
the City and sent
to the *Fietsdepot*

I.v.m. werkzaamheden en/of
op grond van art. 4.2 en/of
4.27 van de apv worden
(brom)-fietsen (ook die aan
brugleuningen en in/aan/om
fietsenrekken) verwijderd.
Sloten worden niet vergoed.
Fiets weg: 21-8-'17
Bel Fietsdepot
020-3344522

GRIMNES.

The City of
Amsterdam removes
bicycles that are illegally
parked, those that appear
to be abandoned, and
those that have not been
used for several weeks (a
warning sticker is placed
on bicycles to tell owners
that they have to remove
their bicycle by a certain
date). To give an idea of
how intensive this pro-
cess is, 64,000 bicycles
were removed by the City
in 2016 alone.[3,24] In certain highly-congested
areas, such as around train stations, and at the Leidseplein and the Van
der Helstplein, bicycles can be parked for a maximum of two weeks, after
which they will be officially removed.[3]

Sometimes, people assume that their bike has been stolen,
when it has actually been taken by the City to the Bicycle Depository (the
Fietsdepot) in the west of Amsterdam, where it is stored for six weeks at the
time of writing. Only about 25% of owners actually reclaim their bikes.[3]

If your bicycle goes missing, it is worth checking whether it is
stored there. You can fill out a form online, including a description of your

bicycle, at www.amsterdam.nl/parkeren-verkeer/fiets/fietsdepot/bicycle-depository-0/, or call them at 020 334 4522. If you pay a fee, it is possible to pick up your bicycle or to have it delivered to you. To prove ownership of your bicycle, bring along your key to show that it fits the lock, as well as your ID.

Objects frequently get stolen from bicycles that are parked in the city centre – from bicycle seat covers, bags, and bicycle lights to tires, saddles, and the entire bicycle itself. While it is possible to go for years without experiencing any theft, it is also possible to come back to the spot where you parked your bicycle, only to find that it is gone. If you are in a hurry or you can keep a close eye on your bicycle, you might be able to get away with leaving it unlocked for a short period of time. Generally speaking, however, it is best to lock it. If you are leaving temporarily, e.g. to nip into a store, you may be able to rely on the wheel lock that clamps the back wheel, assuming that your bicycle is equipped with one. If you are leaving it for an extended period of time, be sure to use a good-quality

Bicycles being taken to the *Fietsdepot*

chain and lock. Pass the chain through the frame of the bicycle, and not just through the spokes of a tire, because a thief could simply remove the tire and walk away with the rest of the bike. Wherever possible, lock your bicycle to something solid that cannot easily be cut through, such as a lamppost, a bicycle stand, a railing, or a tree. Otherwise, a thief could simply lift your bicycle up and walk away with it or load it into a vehicle, regardless of the number and quality of locks you put on it.

It is possible to have your bicycle engraved with a unique 'frame number', at one of several free-of-charge engraving sessions, which are held weekly at various locations around the city.[25] This helps to deter thieves and also increases the likelihood of retrieval, in the case of either removal by the City of Amsterdam or theft. For more information (in Dutch), visit the municipality website: www.amsterdam.nl/parkeren-verkeer/fiets/fietsdepot/data-fiets-graveren/.

Note down identifying details for your bicycle, such as its make, model number, colour, and frame number, in case you need this

information later. You can register and store these details online, at the Bicycle Registry: www.fietsenregister.nl/?content=registreren. If it is worth the expense, you can also install a GPS tracker or a theft prevention chip on your bicycle. You might also consider buying insurance for your bicycle (*fietsverzekering*), in case of damage or theft. The cost of the premiums will depend on factors such as your location and age, and the cost price and age of the bicycle. Make sure to check how much the deductible is, to ensure that it is worth the expense. It is often also possible to insure second-hand bikes.

In case of theft, you can call the police at 0900 8844, or file a police report using an online form (in Dutch): www.politie.nl/aangifte-of-melding-doen/aangifte-van-diefstal-fiets.html. The police department keeps a registry of stolen bicycles, using the frame number or the theft prevention chip number (if available) as identifying information. When stolen bicycles are recovered, this information is used to find the owner. If you have already been successful in claiming insurance for the stolen bicycle, then the insurance company typically becomes the new owner of the recovered bicycle. If the recovered bicycle is in poor condition, it may be destroyed.[26]

Taking your bike on public transport

It is possible to take your bicycle along with you on certain forms of public transport, between designated hours of the day. Bicycles can be taken for free on ferries run by GVB. You can pay a fee of €1.70 (at the time of writing) to take a bicycle onto the Metro (operated by GVB). This is only allowed outside of peak hours (peak hours are defined as being between 7:00 and 9:00 in the morning, and between 16:00 and 18:30 in the evening, from Monday to Friday).[27] If you are caught with a bicycle during peak hours, you will be fined. Certain carriages are designated for bicycles and have a symbol of a bicycle on the door. In practice, passengers occasionally

Bridge railings provide a secure anchor for your bike

Cycling on board
the IJ ferry

Some Metro trains are
equipped with dedicated
bicycle racks

Carrying a bicycle onto the train

bring their cycles into carriages that are not designated for bicycles, particularly if they are in a hurry or the other carriages are full.

You can pay a fee of €6.10 (at the time of writing) to bring a bicycle onto a train operated by NS between the hours of 9:00 to 16:00 and between 18:30 to 6:30 from Monday to Friday, or anytime on weekends, public holidays, and during the entire months of July and August (as these months correspond to the school vacation period).[28] As with the Metro, you are only supposed to bring your bicycle onto designated carriages, indicated by the symbol of a bicycle, but passengers do not always abide by this rule.

Most Metro and train stations have lifts, which make it easy to reach the platform with your bicycle. You may also carry your bicycle up and down the stairs, or take it with you on the escalator or travellator (a flat, often inclined, moving walkway). Some escalators carry a warning sticker, prohibiting commuters from taking their bicycle onto them. Occasionally, however, the lift is out of order and you have no choice. It is common to see people take their bikes on the escalator, regardless of whether it is permitted or not. This takes a little practice, but is fairly easy once you get the hang of it. During an ascent, as you wheel your bicycle onto the escalator and the stairs start to emerge, the bicycle will tilt upwards at an angle, and the handlebars will move closer to your face. Therefore, be ready to place one foot on the step behind you, allowing you to shift your

Bringing a bicycle on the escalator

body slightly backwards and keep a firm stance. Simultaneously, apply the hand brakes and maintain the pressure until you reach the top. The first time you try it, you may feel the instinct to pull your bicycle upward using your arm strength. This is not necessary, as the grip of the tires on the stairs and the application of the brakes will keep it from rolling backwards. Rather, concentrate on keeping your hold on the brakes. Also, keep the bicycle in an upright position. If possible, at the beginning of your ascent, try to position the tires such that they are resting securely on the steps, rather than teetering on the edge of the steps. If you are already ascending and your bicycle is resting on the edge of the steps, then concentrate primarily on holding the brakes down. When you reach the top, remember to let go of the brakes once the stairs straighten out, otherwise you will not move smoothly off the escalator. It is possible to concentrate so hard on braking that you forget to let go again! If your bicycle is very light, or your arms are strong, you may not need to apply the brakes, but simply hold the bike next to you. The same principles apply when descending an escalator.

Bicycles are not allowed on buses or trams, with the sole exception of IJtram 26. IJtram 26 runs from Central Station to the island of IJburg in the east, which would otherwise be inaccessible to cyclists.

Note that all the above rules only apply to non-folding-bikes. If you have a folding bike, you can take it along for free as hand luggage, as long as it is folded up.

Debris on the road

Avoid cycling over glass if possible, as it may puncture your tires. While a lot of refuse is fairly harmless and can be cycled over without incident, try to avoid it if possible as it may be slippery or get stuck to your bicycle. Unless you have a mountain bike with deep treads on the tires, large, unstable objects such as stones and branches are best avoided. When cycling close to branches, be careful that they do not get caught in the spokes of your wheels.

Unexpected noise

Noise can come from numerous sources — including traffic, people, weather phenomena, buildings, and animals. Some sounds can be particularly startling when they are loud and close by, such as a horn or a shout. If you feel your heart beating faster, your body trembling, and your senses on high alert, remember that this reaction is normal. Your safety is top priority — assess the situation and use your instincts and common sense. Do not worry about whether you look composed or flustered, ambivalent or shocked. Make sure that you stay as safe as possible and remove yourself from potential sources of danger.

Vehicles coming close and moving fast

Many of the roads in the city centre are designed to keep cyclists separated from fast-moving traffic. They often have dedicated cycle lanes, either painted onto the road or physically separated from the other lanes by a road divider or a raised path. Many of the canal 'ring roads' are paved with uneven surfaces and punctuated by speed bumps,

Squeezing narrowly past a car

to slow down traffic. Other road users, particularly drivers of large, moto-rised vehicles, are supposed to give cyclists a wide berth to make them feel safer. Occasionally, however, vehicles or motorcyclists may whiz by inches away, at high speed, leaving you rather shaken. Sometimes, they may touch you or brush against you or your bicycle. This experience is often jarring at best, and rarely, if ever, do the drivers stop to apologise or check whether you are alright.

Alcohol and drugs

Drivers of motorised vehicles and cyclists are not permitted to drive under the influence of alcohol or drugs. Your blood alcohol level must not exceed 0.05%.[29,30]

Traffic accidents

One occasionally witnesses collisions and near-collisions, mostly between cyclists. Sometimes this is as minor as an accidental brush between two bicycles, and more rarely, both cyclists end up sprawled across the ground. That said, cycling is widely considered to be relatively safe, and the chances of being in a serious accident are slim. Among European countries and the US, the Netherlands has one of the lowest rates of cyclist fatalities per distance travelled by bicycle.[1,2] This is attributed to the presence of dedicated cycle paths, the careful design of roads and intersections, the high number of cyclists on the roads (pro-viding 'safety in numbers')[31], the decades-long history of cycling in the Netherlands, the high level of traffic safety education amongst local road users, and the generally low speeds of bicyclists.[32] In Amsterdam, approximately 500 cyclists are seriously hurt in a traffic accident each year, resulting in approximately 3-7 deaths amongst cyclists per year, in recent years.[3] Considering the fact that over 223 million trips are made by bicycle annually, this implies that a serious accident takes place on around 0.0002% of bicycle trips. If you are injured, seek help right away – the emergency number for the police or ambulance is 112.

Bad behaviour

Amsterdam attracts visitors of all backgrounds, and unfortunately, it has its fair share of ill-mannered road users. This ranges from drunken tourists who stumble across the road without paying attention to traffic, to people who think that it is funny to shout loudly in your ear in order to try to throw you off balance. Sometimes other road users smoke cigarettes on or along the cycle path, leaving a trail of smoke in their wake. Much of this bad behaviour is a nuisance and extremely rude at best, and can be dangerous, particularly in the crowded city centre where cars, buses, trams, motorcycles, pedestrians and cyclists are moving in every direction.

Remember that your safety is top priority, and that some people are out to cause trouble and are trying their best to pick a fight with a stranger. If your past experiences have tended to be with road users who are generally polite, respectful, and friendly, then encounters with unfriendly or disrespectful people can be extremely unpleasant. Sometimes, it is when you are feeling relaxed and have let your guard down, that such incidents are the most shocking. However, simply being aware that bad behaviour exists and being mentally prepared for it can go a long way. Usually, such occurrences are a matter of bad luck, and as long as you continually strive to be a safe, sensible road user yourself, you need not take such encounters personally.

Reporting an incident

In most situations, to stay as safe as possible, you should try to minimise contact with uncouth people if you meet them. Unless you have hard evidence of their behaviour, it is difficult to bring perpetrators to justice. Nevertheless, if you need to report an incident to the police, or call the fire brigade or an ambulance, you can call the emergency number at 112, or the non-emergency number at 0900 8844. Always remember that the police are there to serve the public, and that you are entitled to call on them for help. The police department itself states that when you are in doubt, it is better to err on the side of caution and call on them to investigate what turns out to be a false alarm, than to expose yourself to danger or miss a chance to help someone in need.

If you encounter discrimination of any kind, including discrimination that is based on race, religion, gender or nationality, you may report the incident to a dedicated anti-discrimination bureau, Discriminatie.nl, at 0900 2354354.

A police officer on her bike

CHAPTER 4

PREDICTING THE BEHAVIOUR OF OTHER ROAD USERS

Defensive cycling

Initially, the road may seem chaotic, with vehicles and road users coming at you from all directions, at different speeds, and punctuated by a blur of road signs and traffic lights. One needs to exercise caution and expect the unexpected. As you gain familiarity with traffic rules and patterns of behaviour, you will come to recognise and understand the motives of others, and learn to predict their actions. The road will become less chaotic, and you will become adept at identifying users who are safe and experienced, or unsafe and inconsiderate. Some abide by traffic rules, while others do not. Regardless of whether they are adhering to or breaking the rules, you will also learn to recognise those who exercise control over what they are doing, and those who do not.

If you spend enough time cycling on the road, you will inevitably encounter unsafe drivers – it is not a question of whether, but when. How, then, can you minimise risk and maximise your personal wellbeing and safety? The key is to gain an understanding not only of how you or others are supposed to behave (in accordance with traffic regulations), but what people actually do and how and why they do it.

You will encounter all kinds of vehicles and users on the road – including but not limited to: cars, vans, trucks, lorries, buses, trams, trains,

Learn to anticipate other people's behaviour

ambulances, trailers, motorcycles, bicycles, mopeds, microcars, pedestrians, skateboarders, rollerbladers, pets, and horse riders. Although their behaviour is as variable as the personalities of the individual, each group of road users tends to exhibit certain behavioural patterns, which calls for a certain range of responses. Hence, the following sections will delve into the characteristics of the most commonly encountered road users. This will help you to adjust your behaviour to the situation – whether that means playing defensive and proceeding with caution, slowing down, stopping completely, or even getting off your bike if necessary.

Motorised vehicles

This section pertains to motorised vehicles that do not travel along rails or tracks, such as cars, vans, trucks, lorries, buses, ambulances, trailers, motorcycles, mopeds, and microcars.

To predict the behaviour of other drivers, it helps to have a basic grasp of road regulations. It can be extremely instructive to read through a handbook on Dutch traffic regulations, which is used by people who are studying for a driver's licence. For example, the Driving Licence B Traffic Regulations Theory Book[33] (published by VekaBest) is a widely-used guide to traffic regulations in the Netherlands, and is available in English. The better acquainted you are with the restrictions that are imposed on other road users, the better you will be able to predict what they are going to do. That said, many cyclists and other road users are not drivers of motorised vehicles themselves, and use the road without ever having read through official rules or guidelines. Furthermore, drivers frequently break the rules or engage in dangerous behaviour. Knowing what other drivers are supposed to do is no guarantee of what they will actually do, but at a minimum, it builds up an expectation of what might happen. This then allows you to recognise hints of trouble when their behaviour deviates from the norm, and adjust your response accordingly.

Right of way

Traffic coming from the right generally has right of way, i.e. you should give way to traffic approaching from the right. Trams are an exception; you must make way for them regardless of whether they approach from the left or the right.

Signalling and turning

Motorised vehicles are supposed to indicate with their lights when they are about to make a turn. You can sometimes use this to guess whether a driver is about to cross paths with you. Note, however, that indicator lights can be faulty and fail to turn on, and drivers may forget to indicate or to turn off their indicators after having made a turn. Hence, you should never rely solely on indicator lights to discern the intentions of other drivers, but take into account their speed and the direction in which they are headed.

Blocked bicycle lanes

Occasionally, you will find another vehicle parked or stopped in the bicycle lane, blocking your path. This is often because the driver is loading or unloading something, or someone is being picked up or dropped off. Sometimes the driver has simply been too lazy to find an official parking spot.

You have several options: if there is space on the road next to the bicycle lane, you could check whether any traffic is approaching and use the car lane if all is clear. If other vehicles are approaching at speed and there is insufficient space between the stopped vehicle and the approaching vehicle, then it is best to slow down and wait behind the stopped vehicle (making sure that it does not move towards you) until the traffic has passed. Generally speaking, when drivers notice that another vehicle is obstructing the bicycle lane, they should slow down in anticipation that you will move onto the section of the road next to the stopped vehicle. However, drivers who are not used to bicycles will not realise this, so do not assume that they will make way for you.

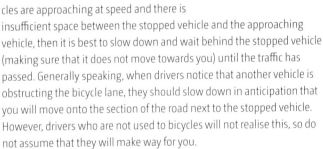

Similarly, at intersections, drivers sometimes misjudge their ability to clear the crossing and end up stopping on the cycle lane. At certain intersections, while attempting to pull out of a junction, drivers sometimes stop on the cycle path in order to gain a clear view of the road. Although they are supposed to try to impede cyclists as little as possible, the cycle lane may be completely or partially blocked. Depending on the situation, cyclists may attempt to go around the vehicle, or wait until the

bicycle lane is clear. Sometimes, when a vehicle is obstructing traffic, the driver may attempt to get out of the way of approaching cars by moving forwards or reversing, and may move onto the bicycle lane in the process. If cyclists are attempting to squeeze past on either side of the vehicle, the driver may be paying attention to only one group of cyclists – either at the front or the back of the vehicle. If the driver decides to reverse or move forward in order to give them more space, the vehicle may inadvertently move towards the other stream of cyclists. It is important to keep these possibilities in mind, and ensure that the vehicle does not hit you.

Lanes of traffic and U-turns

When crossing the road, it is important to look not only in the general direction of the predominant stream of traffic, but also to check the traffic that is coming from other directions, such as from behind you. For example, at an intersection, vehicles may be turning into your path at an angle

Take care that the car does not reverse!

Give way to priority vehicles if their lights and sirens are on

or making a U-turn. Check each lane and do not assume that traffic will be coming from only one direction. Vehicles can reverse suddenly, or move in the wrong direction.

Parked vehicles

A vehicle that is parked may not remain stationary for long; a door may open, a person or an object might emerge from behind it, or the vehicle might start to move. When you pass by a parked vehicle, check whether the lights are on, as that is an indicator of a vehicle that has recently been moving or is about to start moving. Is a driver or occupant present, in the vehicle or near to it? Vehicles such as cars, trucks, buses, and delivery vans are often surrounded by activity – someone is getting in or out, or goods are being transported. If you are unsure, slow down when approaching. If the vehicle is high and it is hard to see what lies beyond, be sure to leave some space between you as you pass. For more information on cycling past parked vehicles, refer to the section on 'Cycling next to parked cars' in Chapter 3.

Priority vehicles
Playing extra defensive

Ambulances, police vehicles, and fire brigades have the right of way if their revolving/flashing lights and two- or three-tone sirens are on. Not only must you give way, it can be extremely dangerous to cross paths with them or obstruct their passage. Hence, you need to be especially alert if you hear such vehicles approaching. Assess the situation, slow down if the emergency vehicle is nearby and it is possible to do so safely, and be prepared to stop if necessary. Keep in mind that other vehicles such as cars will also be trying to work out how to let it pass as safely and smoothly as possible, hence they may engage in unusual behaviour, such as entering into or stopping on the bicycle path, or even the pavement. If the situation is stressful, feel free to stop and get off your bicycle (signalling as needed), and wait in a safe spot until things return to normal.

Cyclists
give way to
the tram

Trams stopped at a
traffic light, leaving
room for the cyclists

Trams

Trams are operated by a human driver, and operate along a subset of roads within the centre. Generally speaking, the separation between the bicycle lane and the tramline is quite distinct, but in certain sections, you may encounter a tram while cycling along a stretch of road that does not have a bicycle lane. If the tram is travelling alongside you and needs to cross your path, you are required to let it pass. If the tram is travelling in the direction of oncoming traffic and needs to cross your path, then you also need to give way. At tram (and rail) crossings, flashing white lights indicate that you can cross, while flashing red lights mean that you have to stop. If a junction is unmarked and you do not have guidance from a traffic light, then you have to give way if the tram is approaching from the left or the right. Note that trams are allowed to run along the Leidsestraat, one of several pedestrian-only streets in Amsterdam. This gives the street the deceptive appearance of being open to vehicular traffic, when in fact, cyclists are banned from riding there.[34]

Tram grooves

Trams run along grooves that are sunk into the ground, and if your bicycle wheel slips inside, it can throw you off balance. Hence, when cycling next to tram grooves, be sure to keep a safe distance, and when crossing them, be sure to do so at an angle. Note that the smooth, metal grooves also become slippery when wet.

Trains

At level crossings for trains and trams, flashing white lights mean that you can cross, while flashing red lights signal that you must stop. Some crossings have barriers that are lowered while a train is passing through. After each train has gone past, the barriers open automatically, even if another train is following close behind. Hence, you should take note of the lights, and never attempt to cross while the light is still red – even if the barriers go up. A sign in Dutch reads, *Wacht tot het rode licht is gedoofd. Er kan nog een trein komen*, meaning, 'Wait until the red light stops flashing. Another train may be approaching'.

Pedestrians

Most local people are used to cyclists. They take care to stay clear of the bike lanes, and will courteously let you pass on a crowded street. Take particular care, though, when cycling next to young children and pets, as their actions may be unpredictable.

Short-term visitors, such as tourists, are unlikely to be fully aware of how the traffic system works, and may not be able to differentiate between a bicycle lane and a pavement for pedestrians. They may walk or stand in the middle of the road or the cycle path, take photographs, or make unexpected movements, such as changing direction abruptly, darting across the road, or raising their arms. Many visitors are accustomed to loud vehicles such as cars and motorcycles, but are easily startled by fast-moving, relatively silent bicycles. You can use your bell to signal your approach, giving them time to react and move out of the way. It is advisable not to expect them to abide by traffic regulations or respect the rules that govern right of way.

Remember that many of them are here on a sightseeing holiday and feel entranced by the cityscape. It might be helpful to imagine your family members and friends in their place. No matter how much of a rush you are in, try to stay patient and slow down, especially if they are clearly oblivious to your presence. While some may jump quickly to the side, others may freeze on the spot, explicitly refuse to make way for you, or even further obstruct your path. Be prepared to slow down to a crawl when you are in a crowded area, and get off your bicycle and walk if necessary. Some pedestrians may be inebriated or 'high' on drugs, with limited control over their actions and mental state. Do not be surprised if you encounter bad behaviour, and remind yourself not to take it personally.

Blind or visually impaired pedestrians can be recognised by a white stick with one or more red rings, and always have priority if they are attempting to cross the road.

Cyclists
Experienced cyclists

In many parts of the world, cycling is typically learnt during one's childhood or youth, sometimes under the guidance of a friend or family member. Many Dutch people, however, have a radically different relationship to bicycles. As soon as children are able to sit upright on their own, many parents use a child seat to transport them by bicycle, so babies and toddlers are already used to the sights and sounds of the bicycle lane.

Tourists enjoy a drink while pedalling through the centre

Cycling through the crowds

Child seats come in various configurations

A trailer is used to transport young children

A *bakfiets* being
used to transport
a young child

121

Babies that
are unable to sit upright
on their own may be
carried in a reclining
basket known as a *baby
mee*, or seated in a child
seat that is attached to a
trailer.[35]

When chil-
dren get slightly older
(around the age of 5),
they may sit on a trailer
bike, which is connected
to their parent's bicycle,
or sit in a *bakfiets*, which
has a wheelbarrow-like
container attached to
the front, and can be
used to hold anything from children and dogs to
furniture and flower pots.

Kids may also ride with their parents
on a tandem bike, which allows them to practice
peddling and get used to balancing on the bike,
while their parents pay attention to their safety.[36]

At almost all of the 225 primary schools
in Amsterdam, students undergo a compulsory
road safety education programme, in which they

Teaching a child to cycle

learn about traffic regulations. Most pupils complete a theory examination at the age of 10-11, and 70% of students subsequently complete a practical examination at the age of 11-12.[3,32]

It may seem intimidating to know that the majority of your fellow cyclists have been 'raised in the saddle'. However, on the bright side, this goes to show that the cycling infrastructure is so well-developed that even young children can travel safely by bike. Furthermore, you may rest assured that the majority of fellow cyclists know what they are doing when on the road.

Carrying a baby
on the bike

Dutch children start cycling
from an early age

Mobile devices and headphones

It is common to see people using their phone and listening to music while cycling.

A survey conducted in the Netherlands estimated that approximately 70% of cyclists use a mobile phone or other portable electronic device while cycling,[37] and it is in fact not illegal to do so (yet). Note, however, that preliminary evidence indicates that high mobile phone usage may be correlated with higher risk of being involved in an accident.[37] If you feel the need to use your phone while cycling, e.g. for GPS navigation, consider mounting a phone holder on your handlebars to free your hands.

An improvised phone holder
for hands-free navigation

One-handed
cycling

126　　　Carrying a stack
of goods on the
front rack

Transporting miscellaneous goods

People transport all kinds of objects by bicycle in Amsterdam, including suitcases, furniture, mattresses, appliances, musical instruments, ladders, large signs, picture frames, animals, plants, and other household items. Objects are often carried under one arm, while the cyclist rides an ordinary two-wheeled bicycle. People also frequently use a *bakfiets*. Occasionally, one sees a cyclist carrying an object with both hands while pedalling.

Transporting children, pets, and other riders

Cyclists can take another rider (or more) on their bicycle, usually seated on a rack on the front or rear of the bike, or sideways on a horizontal crossbar.

Sometimes, the passenger (particularly children and smaller people) stands on the rack over the back tire, with their hands on the cyclist's shoulders for support.

The front rack makes a good seat for an extra rider

Standing on the rear rack

Two children fit comfortably onto the front and rear racks

You will frequently see children being transported by bicycle, at the front and/or the rear of the bike. It is very common to see an adult carrying two or three children on a single bicycle.

Children under the age of 8 must be secured in an approved child seat that supports their back, feet and hands. Foot guards are essential, to prevent their feet from getting caught in the spokes of the wheels.[38] A front windshield can also be used to protect children from the wind and rain. In the Netherlands, it is not compulsory for children to wear a helmet when riding or being carried on a bicycle.

Children with support
guards under their feet

Enjoying the ride
with furry friends

Pets are often transported in bas-
kets or in a *bakfiets*. Dogs, in particular, can
often be seen running alongside their owner's
bicycle, attached to a leash. If you see a dog on
or along the bicycle path, pay extra attention.
The owner will probably appreciate it if you
slow down in anticipation that it might stray
onto your path, especially if it is young and
excitable.

Breaking (or bending) the rules

You will see all kinds of illegal or barely-legal behaviour from cyclists, such as cycling in the wrong direction, cycling in the lane for cars when it is compulsory to use the bicycle lane, cycling along a stretch that is off-limits for cyclists, cycling on the pavement, running red lights, neglecting to signal when turning, and failing to stop for pedestrians at zebra crossings. More rarely, one sees cyclists who are driving under the influence of drugs or alcohol.

The most common infractions often occur for a predictable, if illegal, reason. When cyclists ride in the wrong direction or along prohibited routes, it may be because it is faster or more convenient for them to get to their destination via the 'wrong' side of the road. When cyclists enter car lanes, it may be because the bicycle lane is blocked, or they want to over-take someone. Some cyclists, particularly those on road bikes, prefer the smooth asphalt surface of the road to the bumpier surface of the cycle path. Cyclists sometimes run red lights and whiz through zebra crossings in order to save some time. They may fail to signal their intentions because they forgot, did not think it necessary, or were unable to because they were distracted or their hands were full. Sometimes, their brakes may not be operating properly, preventing them from slowing down in a timely manner. While this does not excuse such behaviour, it allows you to understand it – as well as anticipate it and react to it accordingly.

Sometimes, you will see cyclists who break the rules while continuing to behave in a polite, considerate manner towards others. For example, if they are cycling on the wrong side of the road, and heading in your direction, they may go off the bicycle path and onto the pavement when they see you, in order to clear the way for you. Similarly, if a group of cyclists is cycling more than two abreast and taking up much of the cycle path, some of them may move to the grass or the pavement to get out of your way. As you grow more familiar with the conventions of the road and learn what is commonly encountered behaviour and what is not, you will likely come to recognise such subtleties in behaviour more often.

If you break or bend the rules yourself, be sure to take extra care when doing so, as your behaviour becomes less predictable to others. Do not expect others to give way to you if you do not have the right of way – some people will graciously accommodate you, but others will not. Be prepared to slow down, stop, or move out of the way, and certainly do not do anything that endangers yourself or others unnecessarily.

Road bikers

A road bike is a streamlined, lightweight bicycle that is designed for cycling at high speed. Cyclists on road bikes typically wear protective gear, such as a helmet, and special clothes designed for cycling and made of breathable fabric, such as bicycle pants or shorts. These road users can attain speeds of over 25-30 km/h, whereas the average speed of other cyclists tends to be around 15 km/h. Cyclists on road bikes are hence likely to swiftly over-

Road bikes in the city centre

take others, sometimes passing very close and swerving sharply between fellow cyclists. Some also have a tendency to run red lights or pass quickly in front of other road users. While users of road bikes tend to be highly experienced cyclists, their crouched-over posture and high velocity may sometimes make it harder for them to survey their surroundings and for others to react to them.

Biking on the job

Numerous occupations require the transportation of goods and people – from food delivery and postal services, to the police and the armed forces. Hence, it comes as no surprise that many people ride bicycles as part of their daily business. Food delivery bikers can be identified by a large, often boxy-looking backpack containing food for customers. As they are often in a hurry, one tends to see them riding at high speed, running red lights, cycling in the wrong direction, and swerving into car lanes and across pavements. Although they ride faster than most other cyclists, they are usually on an ordinary bicycle and carry a heavy load, hence they do not go as fast as road bikes.

Post delivery workers are attired in the distinctive orange uniform of PostNL, the national postal service.

Personnel from the police force, as well as from the Dutch military (also known as the Royal Netherlands Marechaussee, or KMar), can be seen patrolling the streets by bike.

A food delivery cyclist in
a brightly coloured outfit

Police- and KMar officers
(military police) on their bikes

Brightly coloured
rental bicycles

Less-experienced cyclists

While the streets are typically dominated by locals and experienced cyclists, there are also plenty of less-experienced road users on bicycles, particularly in the historic centre of Amsterdam. Cycling is often promoted to tourists as an authentic and healthy way to get around and enjoy the city. Numerous shops rent out bicycles, which are often brightly-coloured and emblazoned with the shop's logo. These bicycles are easy to spot, especially when groups of tourists are travelling together on bicycles of the same colour and make.

Some shops also rent out more discreetly-coloured bikes, allowing visitors to blend in with the crowd. Other give-away signs include a very low bicycle seat that allows the cyclist to quickly place their feet on the ground in case of instability; unsteady steering or playful weaving from left to right; jerky or swaying movements; cycling in the middle or on the left side of the bicycle path; screams and laughter; abrupt braking; and cycling speeds that are either too fast or too slow, sometimes due to selection of a suboptimal gear. Be sure to give these riders extra clearance and do not expect them to adhere to the conventions of etiquette described in this book.

Mobility scooters and Cantas

A mobility scooter is a powered scooter that is similar in appearance to a wheelchair, and is designed for people with limited mobility. A Canta is a two-seater microcar of up to 1.1 metres in width, which is classified as a mobility aid. Cantas may be outfitted with special control mechanisms, be equipped to transport a wheelchair, and/or have a built-in wheelchair lift. Mobility scooters and Cantas are allowed on the bicycle path, the pavement, and the road.[39]

Cantas may also drive on the street, if it is safe to do so

Crossing a busy intersection on a mobility scooter

Mopeds, motor-assisted bicycles and motorcycles/motorbikes

A moped is a lightweight vehicle, usually with two or three wheels, but occasionally with four wheels, with either a combustion engine or an electric motor. Mopeds are limited to a speed of 45 km/h. A motor-assisted bicycle is a type of moped that is not allowed to exceed speeds of 25 km/h and has a blue licence plate on the back.

Motorcycles (also known as motorbikes) are all two-wheeled motorised vehicles that are neither mopeds nor vehicles for disabled people, and that are typically designed to reach higher speeds than mopeds. Occasionally, they come with a trailer or a sidecar attached, which have additional wheels.

Speeding, overtaking, and coming too close

By design, motor-equipped vehicles travel at substantially higher speeds than bicycles that are powered by muscle. While motorcycles are usually barred from the cycle lane and use the road together with heavier vehicles, mopeds share much of the same infrastructure (such as certain cycle lanes and traffic lights) with bicycles. Hence, cyclists can expect to be regularly overtaken by mopeds, which may pass by closely, at high speed. Often, one is faced with oncoming mopeds that enter your lane while they are in the process of overtaking cyclists who are travelling in the opposite direction. Moped riders may sometimes underestimate the space required to pass other road users, squeezing in between others and forcing them to slow down. It is also not uncommon for mopeds to overtake a bicycle and then immediately move directly in front of the cyclist, requiring the cyclist to brake to avoid a collision. The best strategy is to play defensive and

anticipate such behaviour, staying calm and keeping as far to the right as possible, while being prepared to brake or slow down.

Noise and fumes

Mopeds with combustion engines tend to produce high levels of noise and fumes. While this is unhealthy and can be stressful, it can hardly be avoided. Fortunately, most of them move at higher speeds than cyclists, and are soon gone again.

Navigating the busy streets on a moped

WEATHER, CLOTHING, AND ROAD CONDITIONS

CHAPTER 5

The weather in Amsterdam is generally cool and mild, occasionally dipping below zero degrees Celsius in the winter, or rising above 30 degrees Celsius in the summer (according to records from the weather station at Schiphol Airport).[40] The monthly average temperature spans a range of around 4 to 19 degrees Celsius throughout the year, depending on the season (with a yearly average of 10.7 degrees Celsius in 2016).[41] This climate is conducive to cycling, as it allows people to commute by bicycle without perspiring too heavily or ruining their clothes. The weather affects your visibility in numerous ways – factors such as rain, mist, fog, snow, hail, and bright sunshine can make it harder to see your surroundings, and this also depends on the time of day. For more information on visibility, refer to the section on 'Visibility' in Chapter 3.

Rain

Amsterdam experiences rain on approximately 130 days per year, with an average annual precipitation of 860 mm in 2016.[42] Rain takes place throughout the year, regardless of the season, and is generally low in intensity, in the form of drizzles or showers. Thunderstorms occur occasionally (on 32 days in 2016).

Roads may become slippery when wet, especially if there are clumps of damp leaves in the way. Take extra care when turning, and slow down if necessary. If you keep the air pressure inside your tires at the lower end of the recommended range, this results in softer tires, which conform better to the road surface, and yield better grip.[43] Due to poor drainage of water, puddles may form on the cycle lane, causing cyclists to swerve around them. When going through large puddles, slow down and/ or lift your feet off the pedals to avoid splashes. If puddles form on the road, cars will inevitably drive through them at speed, splashing adjacent road users. If you want to avoid getting soaked, wear waterproof clothing or try waiting for a gap in the traffic before cycling next to large puddles.

An umbrella keeps the rain off

Wind

Due to its proximity to the North Sea towards the west, Amsterdam experiences prevailing winds from the southwest, with an average wind speed of 11-13 knots.[40] Note that the average wind speed does not necessarily convey the strength of gusts, which can easily be double or triple the average speed.

If you have gears, adjust them to match the strength of the wind. If strong winds are coming from behind, you may be able to move to a higher gear to take advantage of the extra push. If the wind is blowing strongly against you, move to a lower gear to make cycling easier. If the wind is very strong, it can be difficult to make headway. In these cases, you will sometimes see a line of cyclists, positioned one in front of the other in order to save energy. The lead cyclist expends the greatest effort, forming a protective zone which subsequent cyclists can take advantage

Visibility drops
off rapidly in
the mist

of. The stronger the wind, the shorter the distance between the cyclists. If the wind is very strong, you do not need to worry too much about 'tailgating' the cyclist in front of you, as the opposing force of the wind makes it easy to decelerate or stop at short notice.

If you experience strong gusts of wind, take great care when cycling, as you may be buffeted and swept unexpectedly side-ways. Rapid adjustments in steering are required, to keep moving along a straight path.

Low temperatures

Mist

Mist is a fairly frequent occurrence, particularly on the outskirts of the city during the winter season (56 days in 2016).[42] Traffic typically slows down due to the reduced visibility. Adjust your speed accordingly and listen carefully for other road users.

Bridges

Bridges are exposed to cold air from both above and below, hence frost often forms on them before it forms on other road surfaces. Take extra care when cycling across a bridge and if possible, ride over areas that are less icy and slippery.

Snow and ice

Snow comes in numerous forms; light or heavy, dry or wet, fast-melting or slow-melting. The way in which it behaves depends on the surrounding temperature and humidity levels. In 2016, Amsterdam experienced snowfall on 11 days of the year, mostly from January to March and November to December.[42] When the temperature is above zero and/or the snowfall is light, the snow can melt quickly, leaving no more than a thin layer of snow or dampness on the roads. Under these conditions, cycling in light snow is similar cycling in the rain, except that the snow

Cyclists brave the snow and ice

takes longer to melt and soak into your clothes. Visibility is somewhat reduced and road surfaces become slippery.

When temperatures drop below zero, rainwater may freeze, or snow may melt and refreeze. Ice may form over the roads in large sheets or in puddles. Sometimes, such as when temperatures rise above zero again, it becomes both wet and icy, and the road is covered in slush. Take extra care on slippery surfaces, and avoid braking or turning abruptly, as these movements can cause you to lose traction and skid. If water gets inside the cables of your hand brakes or gears, it can freeze and cause them to stop working, particularly after a cold night. You can avoid this by keeping your bicycle indoors, where the temperature is higher.

Stopping and turning

Cycling on snow and ice is extremely different from cycling on ordinary surfaces. While travelling in a straight line, with sufficient momentum to carry you forward, it is possible to cycle fairly smoothly (albeit slowly). However, the lack of grip between the tires and the snow means that turns and stops will quickly cause the tires to lose traction. When the brakes are applied, the tires do not continue to turn but instead start to slide uncontrollably over the ground. In an instant, the tires can slip sideways, causing the bicycle to give out from under you. Hence, if you need to slow down or stop, try to do so over a long distance, and instead of using the brakes, simply stop pedalling and glide to a stop. Note that when you come to a stop, if you are on a slippery surface, the lack of forward momentum can also cause your bicycle to fall over. Similarly, if you try to turn too quickly or at a steep angle, your tires can lose their grip and the tilt of your bicycle cause it to fall over. When attempting a turn, give yourself an extra-large turning radius and keep your bicycle as upright as possible. If you are cycling over a thick layer of snow and there is no other traffic nearby, then at least your falls will be cushioned by the snow and you should still be fairly safe.

Carrying a bicycle along
the frosty road

If a thick-enough layer of snow has formed, then it may obscure the contours of the underlying road surface. It can be hard to distinguish between the cycle lane and the raised pavement, or between the cycle lane and the road. You may find yourself cycling in smooth, pure-white snow, and suddenly falling over because your tire has hit a hidden kerb. Similarly, a layer of snow may hide an underlying layer of ice.

As the snow melts and vehicles drive through it, it may form piles and become compacted until it is solid. For example, if deep ruts have formed in the snow, and the snow continues to freeze and remain solid, then these ruts can be as destabilising as tram grooves or ruts in thick mud. As snow disappears from the main cycle paths and roads, the remaining snow may form mounds on the corners of junctions or pavements.

Hail

Hailstones are formed when droplets of water freeze into solid balls that rain down and sometimes strike the skin painfully. In the Netherlands, hailstones are rarely very big, and tend not to be too disruptive to cyclists, as long as one wears adequate clothing. They typically roll off your clothes before they melt, leaving you relatively dry.

Cycling through
the hail

Jackets and hoods
offer protection
from light drizzles

Clothing

When the temperature drops or the weather turns bad,
Amsterdammers often continue to wear 'ordinary' clothing such as jackets and coats when commuting for short distances by bike. You quite often see cyclists carrying umbrellas to protect themselves from the rain. For longer journeys, people typically wear raincoats or waterproof clothing.

If you are covering substantial distances by bike, consider investing in a few items that will protect you from the elements. Waterproof and windproof clothing, such as a jacket (*regenjas*) and pants (*regenbroek*), can be bought separately, or as a suit (*regenpak*). A thermal fleece, worn under your jacket, will help to reduce the chilling effect of the wind and surround your body with an insulating layer of warm air. Light, modern fabrics allow the skin to keep breathing, while wicking away moisture and perspiration. Although you may feel cold at the start of your ride, you are likely to warm up while cycling. Some jackets have zippered panels, allowing air to circulate and enabling you to regulate your temperature over the course of your ride. A one-piece rain coat (*regenponcho*) will protect most of your body from the rain, but may also increase your surface area and slow you down when the wind is strong. Leg covers ('rainlegs') are waterproof or water-resistant coverings for the upper legs (as opposed to pants), to keep your thighs dry during light-to-moderate rain.

Depending on the temperature, you may want to wear gloves, ranging from light 'fashion' gloves to heavy-duty waterproof gloves during the rainy or icy season. When temperatures drop to zero and below, you may need to wear a glove liner or two nested pairs of gloves. If you need an extra source of heating, you can place hand warmers inside your gloves. These may come in the form of reusable hand warmers, which need to be soaked in hot water prior to use, or single-use hand warmers, which produce heat through a chemical reaction upon exposure to the air.

Thick clothing keeps this cyclist
warm in the winter

FINAL WORDS

Now that you have reached the end of this guidebook, my final message to you is to cycle as often as possible, and to keep practicing and working on your cycling skills. Soon enough, you will notice the difference and marvel at your progress on the road. Stay safe, breathe, and remember to have fun! I wish you all the best in your cycling adventures, and many enjoyable rides through the beautiful city of Amsterdam!

ACKNOWLEDGEMENTS

I would like to give my heartfelt thanks to the many people who contributed to this book, in one way or another. Many thanks, first and foremost, to my publisher at XPat Media, Bert van Essen, for believing in this project, drawing upon a wealth of resources and enthusiasm, and turning it into reality. Huge thanks goes to my designer and layout editor, Bram Vandenberge, for doing a beautiful job and accommodating my many requests and edits. My great appreciation goes to Stephanie Dijkstra, editor-in-chief at The XPat Journal, for proofreading and fine-tuning the manuscript. Warm thanks go to my talented photographers, Kevin McPeake and Shirley Agudo, for their creative and vivid images, which bring the text to life. My deep gratitude goes to my anonymous adviser from the *Fietsersbond*, for proofreading my manuscript and providing extensive feedback and suggestions for improvement. To Janne Rijkers from the Auteursbond, thank you for taking the time and energy to provide me with legal advice. A big thank you goes to my wonderful and inspiring friends, who brainstormed with me, provided feedback on the concept and manuscript, and supported and encouraged me throughout the process – Christian Bach, Dirk de Jong, Emma Fitzgerald, Jessica Hsia, and Caspar van Lissa. Special thanks goes to my friends Aga Wislanski and Tim Bleeker for their constant generosity and support, and immense help with the photography. Last but not least, the biggest thank you goes to my parents, Tan Mui Siang and Chin Oi Tow, and my aunt, Tan Mui Sung, who gave me my lifelong passions for reading, writing, drawing, observation, and above all, artistic and creative expression.

REFERENCES

1. Pucher, J. & Buehler, R. Cycling for Everyone: Lessons from Europe. *Transportation Research Record Journal of the Transportation Research Board* **2074,** 58–65 (2008).

2. Pucher, J. & Dijkstra, L. Promoting Safe Walking and Cycling to Improve Public Health: Lessons From The Netherlands and Germany. *American Journal of Public Health* **93,** 1509–1516 (2003).

3. I amsterdam. FAQ Cycling in Amsterdam. *iamsterdam.com* (2014). at www.iamsterdam.com/en/our-network/media-centre/city-hall/dossier-cycling/cycling-faq

4. Agudo, S. *The Dutch and Their Bikes.* (XPat Scriptum Publishers, 2014).

5. O'Sullivan, F. Amsterdam Has Officially Run Out of Spaces to Park Its Bicycles. *citylab.com* (2015). at www.citylab.com/commute/2015/02/amsterdam-has-officially-run-out-of-spaces-to-park-its-bicycles/385867/

6. Press, T. A. (Hz) Netherlands Bicycle Fishing. *aparchive.com* (2011). at www.aparchive.com/metadata/-HZ-Netherlands-Bicycle-Fishing/cc7d792e143f5bfec66aac79907d4b8f

7. Boute, C. CycleSpace puts a new spin on cycling. *Hello Zuidas* (2017).

8. Fietsambassade CycleSpace naar Zuidas. (2017). at www.amsterdam.nl/zuidas/nieuws/2017/maart/fietsambassade/

9. CycleSpace. Anna Luten is Bicycle Mayor 2016! *cyclespace.nl* at http://cyclespace.nl/bicyclemayor/

10. O'Sullivan, F. Amsterdam Is Appointing a Bike Mayor. *citylab.com* (2016). at www.citylab.com/solutions/2016/04/amsterdam-is-appointing-a-bike-mayor/479901/

11. Oja, P. *et al.* Health benefits of cycling: a systematic review. *Scandinavian Journal of Medicine & Science in Sports* **21,** 496–509 (2011).

12. Fishman, E., Schepers, P. & Kamphuis, C. B. M. Dutch Cycling: Quantifying the Health and Related Economic Benefits. *American Journal of Public Health* **105,** 1–3 (2015).

13   I amsterdam. Bikes in Amsterdam. *iamsterdam.com* (2017). at
     www.iamsterdam.com/en/local/about-amsterdam/transportation/bikes

14   Mccormack, L. How to Achieve the Perfect Bike Tire Pressure. (2010). at
     www.bicycling.com/maintenance/tires/yourtires-air

15   Fietsersbond. Slotentest - Fietsersbond. *fietsersbond.nl* (2017). at
     www.fietsersbond.nl/de-fiets/onderdelen/sloten/slotentest/

16   Ministry of Infrastructure and the Environment. *Road Traffic Signs and
     Regulations in the Netherlands*. 1–80 (Ministry of Infrastructure and the
     Environment, 2014).

17   De Rijksoverheid. Fiets. *rijksoverheid.nl* at www.rijksoverheid.nl/onderwer-
     pen/fiets

18   Bicycle Dutch. Road signs for cycling in the Netherlands. *bicycledutch.
     wordpress.com* (2012). at https://bicycledutch.wordpress.com/2012/06/04/
     road-signs-for-cycling-in-the-netherlands/

19   Fiets Telweek. Resultaten Fiets Telweek bekend! *fietstelweek.nl* (2016).
     at http://fietstelweek.nl/resultaten-fiets-telweek-bekend/

20   I amsterdam. Amsterdam's cycling history. *iamsterdam.com* (2017). at
     www.iamsterdam.com/en/visiting/plan-your-trip/getting-around/cycling/
     amsterdam-cycling-history

21   Staples, H. & Staples, S. Parking your bicycle in Amsterdam. *holland-cycling.
     com* (2017). at www.holland-cycling.com/amsterdam/getting-around-
     amsterdam/parking-your-bicycle-amsterdam

22   Gemeente Amsterdam. Fietsenstallingen. *amsterdam.nl* (2017). at
     www.amsterdam.nl/parkeren-verkeer/fiets/fietsparkeren/

23   Stalling Amsterdam. Stalling Amsterdam. *stallingamsterdam.nl* (2017). at
     www.stallingamsterdam.nl/pub/stalling/index.php

24   RTL Nieuws. Fietsersbond: Hou op met wegknippen fietsen. *rtlnieuws.nl*
     (2014). at www.rtlnieuws.nl/nieuws/binnenland/fietsersbond-hou-op-met-
     wegknippen-fietsen

25   I amsterdam. Data fiets graveren. (2017). at www.amsterdam.nl/parkeren-
     verkeer/fiets/fietsdepot/data-fiets-graveren/

26   De Rijksoverheid. 8 vragen en antwoorden over Fiets. *rijksoverheid.nl* at
     www.rijksoverheid.nl/onderwerpen/fiets/vraag-en-antwoord

27   GVB. Bicycle ticket (Bicycle supplement). *gvb.nl* at https://en.gvb.nl/fiets-
     kaartje-supplement-fiets

28   NS. Day ticket bicycle. *ns.nl* (2017). at www.ns.nl/producten/en/alleen-te-

koop-via-station-of-kaartautomaat/p/dagkaart-fiets

29 de Waard, D., Houwing, S., Ben Lewis-Evans, Twisk, D. & Brookhuis, K. Bicycling under the influence of alcohol. *Transportation Research Part F: Psychology and Behaviour* **41,** 302–308 (2016).

30 OECD/ITF. *Road Safety Annual Report 2016.* 1–540 (OECD Publishing, 2016). doi:http://dx.doi.org/10.1787/irtad-2016-en

31 Jacobsen, P. L. Safety in numbers: more walkers and bicyclists, safer walking and bicycling. *Injury Prevention* **9,** 205–209 (2003).

32 Schepers, P., Twisk, D., Fishman, E., Fyhri, A. & Jensen, A. The Dutch road to a high level of cycling safety. *Safety Science* **92,** 264–273 (2017).

33 VekaBest Verkeersleermiddelen BV. *Driving Licence B Traffic Regulations Theory Book.* (Maklu, 2015).

34 de Fietsersbond. Van 'fietsendorado' tot fietsvrij: 50 jaar fietsverbod Leidse-straat. *Op eigen kracht* **82,** 7–8 (2010).

35 Bicycle Dutch. Cycling with a baby. *bicycledutch.wordpress.com* (2013). at https://bicycledutch.wordpress.com/2013/07/04/cycling-with-a-baby/

36 Staples, H. & Staples, S. Cycling with children. *holland-cycling.com* (2017). at www.holland-cycling.com/tips-and-info/cycling-with-children

37 Goldenbeld, C., Houtenbos, M., Ehlers, E. & De Waard, D. The use and risk of portable electronic devices while cycling among different age groups. *Journal of Safety Research* **43,** 1–8 (2012).

38 Sturms, L. M. in *Pediatric traffic injuries* 101–112 (Pediatric traffic injuries, 2013).

39 De Rijksoverheid. Rijden met een scootmobiel. *regelhulp.nl* at www.regel-hulp.nl/bladeren/_/artikel/rijden-met-een-scootmobiel/

40 Windfinder. *Wind and weather statistics: Amsterdam-Schiphol Airport.* at www.windfinder.com/windstatistics/amsterdam-schiphol

41 Royal Netherlands Meteorological Institute. Maand- en jaarwaarden. *knmi.nl* (2017). at www.knmi.nl/nederland-nu/klimatologie/maandgegevens

42 Royal Netherlands Meteorological Institute. *Jaaroverzicht van het weer in Nederland 2016.* 1–17 (2017).

43 Road Bike Tire Pressure - Get It Right! - I Love Bicycling. (2014). at www.ilovebicycling.com/road-bike-tire-pressure-get-it-right/